GERMAN COMMAND HEADQUARTERS IN THE WEST

HITLER'S COMMANDERS AT OB. WEST

THEN AND NOW

GERMAN COMMAND HEADQUARTERS IN THE WEST

HITLER'S COMMANDERS AT OB. WEST

THEN AND NOW

by Jean Paul Pallud

AFTER THE BATTLE

An Imprint of Pen & Sword Books Ltd

FSC
www.fsc.org
MIX
Paper | Supporting responsible forestry
FSC® C122244

German Command Headquarters in the West – Then and Now

Published by After the Battle
An imprint of Pen & Sword Books Ltd
47 Church Street, Barnsley,
South Yorkshire, S70 2AS
Tel. 01226 734222
Fax. 01226 734438
Email: enquiries@pen-and-sword.co.uk
Website: **www.afterthebattle.com**
www.pen-and-sword.co.uk

Printed and bound in India by Parksons Graphics Pvt. Ltd.

ISBN: 9781036126780

Commissioning Editor: Rob Green
Editor: Jean Paul Pallud
Design: Paul Wilkinson
Cover design: Jon Wilkinson

Credits:
The major part of this book was originally published as an article in *After the Battle* magazine: 'The Ob. West at Saint-Germain-en-Laye' by Jean Paul Pallud in issue 141 (August 2008). It has been adapted and enhanced to produce this book and additional photos are included.

Acknowledgements:
The Editor would like to acknowledge the late Henri de Rolland for his support. The Editor would also like to acknowledge Denis Bamps, Bruno Renoult, and Patrick Périn, the then Director of the Musée d'Archéologie Nationale at Saint-Germain-en-Laye.

Photo Credit Abbreviations:
BA – Bundesarchiv; ECPAD – Médiathèque de la Défense, Fort d'Ivry; USNA – US National Archives. Unless specified otherwise, all illustrations are from the After the Battle archive.

Front Cover: The huge Ob. West bunker at Saint-Germain-en-Laye comprised three blocks and measured more than 60 metres long. It provided about 40 rooms, or more than 60 if passages, corridors, and toilets are included.

Back Cover:
Top: Most of the Ob. West staff moved to hotels in Paris during the winter months, particularly to the Hôtel George V. This hotel and the one next door, the Prince de Galles, also served as convenient locations for major meetings or conferences, even in the summer months. Then and Now in front of the Hôtel Prince de Galles, with the Hôtel George V in left background. (BA and ATB)

Centre: On May 8, 1944, von Rundstedt called for a top-level conference at the Prince de Galles. L-R: General der Panzertruppen Geyr von Schweppenburg, Generaloberst Blaskowitz, Generalfeldmarschall Sperrle, von Rundstedt, Rommel, and Admiral Krancke. (BA)

Bottom: Von Rundstedt was relieved of his command at the beginning of July 1944 and Generalfeldmarschall Günther von Kluge then assumed command of Ob. West. Then and Now at the Villa David, today the office of the Collège Marcel Roby, Rue La Rochejaquelein. (BA and ATB)

CONTENTS

Once again appointed Ob. West after von Witzleben left command in March 1942, von Rundstedt was relieved again in early July 1944 and Generalfeldmarschall Günther von Kluge then took command of the Ob. West. Von Kluge moved into the offices that von Rundstedt occupied in the Villa David. (BA)

INTRODUCTION

AFTER SEVEN MONTHS OF 'Phoney War', the Wehrmacht launched its attack in the West on May 10, 1940 and within six weeks the Netherlands, Belgium and France had been defeated, and the British Expeditionary Force evacuated in haste. The armistice with France was signed on June 22 and hostilities ceased three days later.

Of the three army groups that had fought and won the swift campaign, Heeresgruppe A was designated to remain in the West and Generalfeldmarschall Gerd von Rundstedt and his staff soon established themselves at Saint-Germain-en-Laye, just west of Paris. By July it was clear that Britain intended to keep on fighting so Hitler ordered his army and navy staffs to plan for the invasion of Great Britain. On September 5, Heeresgruppe A drew up the provisional instructions for Operation 'Seelöwe' which would involve two armies – the 9. Armee and 16. Armee – and defined the two waves of the assault. On September 14, Heeresgruppe A issued its Order No. 1 for 'Seelöwe' and on the 25th Generaloberst Franz Halder, Chief of the General Staff at the Oberkommando des Heeres (OKH, the Army High Command), came in person to the headquarters at Saint-Germain for a map exercise. This confirmed his view that the main attack should be carried by the 16. Armee on the right wing.

Apart from the continuing lack of air superiority over southern England, it was equally apparent that there was insufficient shipping available to carry the Wehrmacht across the Channel. The Kriegsmarine strongly recommended against the operation and on October 12 Hitler decided to postpone 'Seelöwe' until the following spring. In his book *Von Rundstedt, the soldier and the man* published in 1952, Günther Blumentritt (in 1940 the Operations Officer at Heeresgruppe A) wrote that from the beginning von Rundstedt and his staff always thought that the operation would never be launched.

Hitler had by then decided to attack the Soviet Union and, to enable the OKH to devote its attention to planning that campaign in the East, on October 29 Heeresgruppe A was designated theatre commander for the West and Generalfeldmarschall von Rundstedt, was appointed Commander-in-Chief West (Oberbefehlshaber West or Ob. West for short) and made responsible for all the German-occupied territory in western Europe. He was placed directly under the Oberkommando der Wehrmacht (OKW, Armed Forces High Command).

Jean Paul Pallud

Von Kluge was in turn relieved on August 16 and Generalfeldmarschall Walter Model arrived on the night of the 17th to take over as fifth Ob. West at Saint-Germain. This photo was taken on August 26 in Metz-en-Couture, south-east of Saint-Quentin, after the withdrawal of Model and his staff from Saint-Germain. Though it was a very difficult time, the German commanders paused to smile at the ceremony of awarding the Knight's Cross to Oberst Rudolf-Christoph von Gersdorff (second from left), the chief-of-staff of General der Panzertruppen Heinrich Eberbach (right), commander of the 7. Armee. On the left was SS-Oberstgruppenführer Joseph Dietrich, commander of the 5. Panzerarmee. The leaders of the 11th Armoured Division would surprise Eberbach in Saleux five days after this photo was taken, and he was captured. (Munin Verlag)

THE OB. WEST AT SAINT-GERMAIN-EN-LAYE

WHEN THEY FIRST ARRIVED at Saint-Germain in late June 1940, von Rundstedt and his staff had set up their quarters in the Pavillon Henri IV at the southern end of the majestic terraces that overlook the Seine River and Paris. All that remains of the Château Neuf built by King Henri IV of France, the location was undoubtedly a historic one as it was here that Louis XIV was born and spent his youth, and where his father Louis XIII had died.

The various offices of Ob. West soon took over local schools, such as the Lycée de Jeunes Filles, the École Normale and the École Saint-Érembert, and a barracks, the Quartier Gramont. More villas and apartments were requisitioned to house officers, in the Cité Médicis near the Château, in the Rue Thiers and in Rue de Lorraine.

During the winter months, however, most of the Ob. West staff moved to Paris to the Hôtel George V and other nearby hotels. Generalmajor Günther Blumentritt, by then Chief-of-Staff of Ob. West, explains that this was due to the shortage of coal for heating whereas the Paris hotels cost less to heat. In the spring everyone returned to Saint-Germain. Von Rundstedt disliked the stay in Paris, particularly during holiday periods when people packed the streets, and he wrote to his wife how he longed to return to the peacefulness of Saint-Germain.

Blumentritt later recalled how the Field-Marshal, a garden-lover, had long talks with the old French gardener and how each day at 4.30 p.m. he would receive his staff officers to take tea in the sun in the garden.

Initially, security measures were lax at Saint-Germain and, according to Blumentritt, von Rundstedt's villa was not even cordoned off and there were practically no guards. 'Von Rundstedt did not want that'. Security measures were equally low-key around the headquarters' offices at the Pavillon Henri IV, with no barriers or fencing and no access restrictions. Everyone was just allowed to come and go, French and Germans alike.

'Never carrying any weapon, accompanied only by his adjutant, the Field-Marshal would take his walk of around one to two hours in the morning through Saint-Germain and in the city park. An attempt to have him unostentatiously shadowed by two German detectives met with no success. Von Rundstedt immediately noticed that two men were following at a distance and jokingly referred to them as hangers-on. He then took to the paths of the park and suddenly disappeared round the corner into the wood. Great was his satisfaction when his two watchers could no longer trace him.

In April 1941, when von Rundstedt and his staff were secretly moved to the East for Operation 'Barbarossa', the function of Ob. West was taken over by Generalfeldmarschall Erwin von Witzleben. At first, I was confident that this series of photos was showing the actual take-over between the two field-marshals, and that it had been taken at Saint-Germain-en-Laye. However, when investigating on the spot, it became clear that this was not so. (BA)

I then discovered that these photos had been taken in another famous castle, that of Vaux-le-Vicomte, located near Melun, 55 kilometres south-east of Paris. It was March 1941, during a party to celebrate von Witzleben's 40 years in the army. Holding his field-marshal's baton, von Witzleben inspected an honour company lined up for him in the château garden. (BA)

Such walks often led to amusing incidents. As a rule, the Field-Marshal had chocolate in his pocket for the children, as they very well knew, since these walks took place regularly. He often met the mayor, with whom he was acquainted, or the Abbé from the monastery, or perhaps some French officer in mufti. With a polite greeting von Rundstedt used to step off the pavement into the road, but the approaching figure would do the same! They would then bump into one another in the roadway.'

Von Rundstedt refused to have any kind of shelter constructed in the garden of his villa, remarking to Blumentritt: 'One can be killed just as comfortably in bed as in the cellar'. Consequently, though 'any small bomb could have destroyed the whole house', there was no refuge in case of air raids. The protection of the Ob. West headquarters against air attack was light at that time, Blumentritt recalling only a few 20mm anti-aircraft guns. He explained how the local population was convinced that the Germans had done what should be done to protect their Field-Marshal and that it was confidently said in the city that the presence of von Rundstedt was the 'best anti-aircraft protection'.

Unfortunately, these photos show very little of the grandeur of the garden designed by 17th-century landscape architect André Le Nôtre, a balanced composition of patterned flower-beds, water basins, fountains, and canals.

Vaux-le-Vicomte château was built in 1658-61 for Nicolas Fouquet, the superintendent of finances of King Louis XIV, and is one of Europe's finest constructions of its kind. Fouquet owed his success as Minister of Finance to his brilliant intelligence, and his loyalty to the throne. Many envied him and finally succeeded in making the King believe that his minister's splendour was funded by misappropriation of public funds and in September 1661, a few weeks after the festive opening of his château, Fouquet was arrested by d'Artagnan, captain of the King's musketeers. He stayed incarcerated under close surveillance until his death in March 1680. Vaux-le-Vicomte, from which Louis XIV took his inspiration to build Versailles, remains as his legacy. The German party took place in the central Grand Salon which rises the full height of the château under a dome. (BA)

It was in this same salon that TV actress and *Desperate Housewives* star Eva Longoria and basketball celebrity Tony Parker held their wedding reception on July 7, 2007. They had booked the château for two days and *OK Magazine* paid two million dollars for exclusive photos.

The party then had a meal in another luxurious salon of the château. Von Witzleben addressed his guests, among them in the forefront Generalfeldmarschall Hugo Sperrle, commander of the Luftwaffe in the West, and General der Infanterie Otto von Stülpnagel, the Military Governor of France. (BA)

No banquet today in the Salon Carré but an endless stream of fascinated visitors. All rooms of the château are furnished and open to the public and thousands of tourists flock to view its ornate treasures every year.

Then and Now, in the Chambre du Roi at Vaux-le-Vicomte. (BA and ATB)

Oberst Bodo Zimmermann, the Ob. West Operations Officer, later recalled an anecdote that von Rundstedt personally recounted with a smile in the officers' mess: 'It was his custom each day to take a walk through the streets of Saint-Germain, alone and armed only with his walking stick. The air raid sirens howled. The Field-Marshal, as usual, took no notice. Nor did an elderly French housewife whom he passed, her shopping basket on her arm. "But, Madame", von Rundstedt enquired, "are you not frightened of the bombs?" The old lady replied: "Why should I be afraid, Maréchal, they will not bomb Saint-Germain. It has no military importance, for nothing ever happens here".'

Von Witzleben and Sperrle. Von Witzleben left his command in March 1942, officially for health reasons but sources indicate that he was forcibly retired for criticising the regime. A leading conspirator in the plot to assassinate Hitler, he was designated to become Commander-in-Chief of the Wehrmacht had the plot succeeded. In the evening of July 20, 1944, he went to the Bendlerstrasse block, the General Army Office of the Wehrmacht High Command, in Berlin to take this command but he quickly saw that things were going wrong and left at 8.15 p.m., knowing that the attempt to kill Hitler had failed. He simply returned home where he was soon arrested. Part of the first group of conspirators to be brought before the People's Court on August 7, he was sentenced to death and hanged at Plötzensee Prison on the 8th. (BA)

The town of Saint-Germain-en-Laye dates from the 11th century when Robert II the Pious built a monastery dedicated to Saint Germain. The surrounding forest became a favoured hunting ground for the kings of France and in 1124, King Louis VI had a royal residence built. It was destroyed by the English during the Hundred Years' War but King Charles V rebuilt it and turned it into a fortress. In the summer of 1940, the Oberbefehlshaber West (German Commander-in-Chief in the West) established headquarters at Saint-Germain-en-Laye. A local photographer pictured a German wire obstacle barring access to the Château Vieux on the park side. (Maurice Veillon)

King Henri II decided to build a new castle on the slope overlooking the Seine, and construction was completed in 1600 during the reign of King Henri IV. The Château Neuf deployed two long symmetrical wings on the Seine side which ended in pavilions, while seven successive terraces descended to the river, each connected by elaborate staircases and ramps. King Louis XIV was born there in 1638 (the city's coat of arms features a cradle and his birth date) and he chose the city as his principal residence until 1682 when he moved his court to Versailles. All that remains today of the Château Neuf is the Pavillon Henri IV where Louis XIV was born, and two ramps of a terrace. This painting by Auguste-Alexandre Guillaumot represents the Château Neuf as it was in 1637; in the background, the Château Vieux. The Ob. West headquarters was first established at the Pavillon Henri IV. (BNF, Gallica)

There was another German command established in Saint-Germain: the Militär-Verwaltungs-Bezirk A, responsible for controlling the occupied French territory in region A. It was not subordinated to the Ob. West but to the Militärbefehlshaber Frankreich. The Militärbefehlshaber Frankreich, under General von Stülpnagel, had five geographic commands, Bezirke A, B, C, Bordeaux and Grand-Paris, and specialised commands such as a Propaganda-Abteilung. Then and Now, the establishment was and still is a teacher training school on Rue du Président Roosevelt. (B. Renoult)

On the night of March 3/4, 1942, RAF Bomber Command attacked the Renault factory at Boulogne-Billancourt. Some stray bombs fell at Saint-Germain, one badly damaging the house facing the Pavillon Henri IV, which itself also suffered some damage. In April, other raids again hit the Ford factory and the Camp des Loges, a military camp situated in the forest near Saint-Germain.

Standing as the cornerstone of the long terraces overlooking the Seine valley, the Pavillon Henri IV was an easy target for the RAF so Ob. West finally moved into other buildings in the city.

In April 1941 the headquarters of Heeresgruppe A was secretly moved to the East under the code-name 'Abschnittstab Winter' (on the day of the attack on the Soviet Union, it would take command of the right wing of the front under the new title of Heeresgruppe Süd). Meanwhile in the West, the function of Ob. West was taken over from April 15 by the headquarters of Heeresgruppe D. The new Commander-in-Chief in the West was Generalfeldmarschall Erwin von Witzleben who had three armies under his command, the 15. Armee and 7. Armee manning the coastline from Antwerp to the Spanish border and the 1. Armee in charge of the occupied portion of France.

In December 1941, at his request and for health reasons, von Rundstedt was relieved from command of Heeresgruppe Süd. In March 1942 von Witzleben took leave of his command in the West due to ill health and von Rundstedt took over, being appointed acting commander of Heeresgruppe D and Commander-in-Chief in the West from March 8. He returned to Saint-Germain-en-Laye and his position was made permanent on May 1 although letters to his wife make clear that he was not particularly happy to return

Ob. West headquarters consisted mainly of administrative and communications services and there was a particularly large contingent of German female auxiliaries at Saint-Germain. The French nicknamed these girls the 'souris grises' (grey mice) after the colour of the uniform worn by those serving with the Luftwaffe. This photo had been taken at No. 32 Rue d'Alsace.

This snapshot of Ob. West officers chatting in the street was taken by a member of the German staff for his private photo album.

The location, on Boulevard Victor Hugo, could hardly be more appropriate, being right between the Lycée de Jeunes Filles occupied by the Ob. West headquarters (off to the right) and the command bunker (behind the wall on the left).

to active service. However, von Witzleben's health problems were real (he had to have an operation) but Hitler used them as a convenient pretext to get rid of him as he had never been a supporter of the Nazi regime. After his recovery, von Witzleben was put in the OKH Führer-Reserve, a pool of officers unassigned but on active duty.

Two weeks later, Hitler issued his Führer Directive No. 40 covering the conduct of the defence of the West. He decreed that the defences along the coast should be organised in such a way that any invasion attempt could be

On the night of March 3/4, 1942, RAF Bomber Command sent 235 bombers to attack the Renault factory at Boulogne-Billancourt. About 450 tons of explosives were dropped, destroying 40 per cent of the factory, but many bombs fell astray, killing 367 French people. At Saint-Germain one stray bomb struck the house standing in front of the Pavillon Henri IV.

The house was so badly damaged that it was never repaired and the empty plot is now used as a car park for the hotel. Our comparison is angled slightly to the left to show the position of the Pavillon Henri IV.

broken up either before the actual landing or certainly immediately after. Strong defences were to be built in locations suitable for an enemy invasion, and sectors in danger of small-scale attacks were to be defended by a series of strong points. Other less-vulnerable parts of the coast were to be patrolled.

In 1943 word reached Hitler that his Commander-in-Chief in the West was without air protection of any kind. The Führer reacted immediately and Blumentritt received the order to see to it that adequate shelter was provided forthwith.

Blumentritt: 'Since Hitler knew of the Field-Marshal's refusal, he entrusted the Organisation Todt with the task and instructed them to report to him. The matter now had to be handled carefully. When von Rundstedt went on leave to Bad Tölz in 1943 everything had been prepared so that a

One of those who visited Ob. West at Saint-Germain was General Oshima Hiroshi, the Japanese ambassador in Berlin. An ardent supporter of the Nazi ideology, Oshima met Hitler periodically and thus had an unparalleled access to German war plans and policies. He made visits to the Russian Front, the Atlantic Wall, and German factories, and reported his knowledge in detailed memoranda which he radioed to Tokyo in the 'Purple' diplomatic cipher. Unknown to the Japanese, this code had been broken by the Americans in 1940 and Oshima's reports, with all their factual data, were being read by them almost as soon as he sent them. (BA)

In November 1943, Oshima made a four-day tour of the Atlantic Wall fortifications. At Saint-Germain-en-Laye, from the stone terrace – the outstanding feature of the park designed by André Le Nôtre – he is shown the magnificent view over the Seine valley as far as Paris. Upon his return to Berlin, he wrote a fulsome 20-page report giving the location of every German division, as well as stating its manpower and weaponry. He also described tank ditches, armament of coastal bunkers and available mobile forces. Just one week before D-Day, following a talk with Hitler, Oshima dutifully reported to Tokyo (and to the American code-breakers) that the bulk of the German forces would not be in Normandy, where a diversionary feint by the Allied armies was expected, but in the Pas-de-Calais area where the main strike was suspected to come. (BA)

My grandson Léo played the part for this timeless comparison at the orientation table.

For years, the place where the German Commander-in-Chief in the West had been quartered at Saint-Germain was lost to history. Then in 1993 I discovered an uncaptioned series of photos in the Bundesarchiv showing Generaloberst Heinz Guderian, the Inspector-General of the Armoured Forces, visiting von Rundstedt at his HQ in France. Exploring Saint-Germain with these photographs, I was then able to place them at the Villa David, today the office of the Collège Marcel Roby at No. 3 Rue La Rochejaquelein. (BA and ATB)

Returning from a stroll in the villa garden, von Rundstedt, his Chief-of-Staff General Günther Blumentritt, and Guderian pause for a chat. Despite this irrefutable proof, owners of other houses continued to claim that theirs was the real von Rundstedt villa, but the various known series of photos, both of him and of his successor von Kluge, at Saint-Germain were all taken at the Villa David. (BA and ATB)

The photos with Guderian date from April 1944 when he came to France to try to solve the strategic disagreement between von Rundstedt and Rommel. He himself mainly shared von Rundstedt's views. (BA and ATB)

makeshift shelter in the cellar of the villa could be started on immediately. Thus, when his leave was up, the air raid shelter in the cellar was ready. But this still did not satisfy Hitler and he ordered that an underground bunker should be constructed in the garden, which would be connected to the villa underground, and again an occasion when von Rundstedt went on leave had to be seized. The main anxiety was to spoil the sacred garden as little as possible by this work. This proved successful, thanks to the scrupulous care taken by the engineers and workmen, for it was known that von Rundstedt would be very annoyed if the trees or lawns were spoilt, apart from the fact that he was no lover of concrete. But a privet hedge was damaged and I heard about it in no uncertain terms every time the Commander-in-Chief passed this spot.'

Oberst Zimmermann later recalled that when von Rundstedt returned and saw the air raid shelter, he declared quite categorically that nothing would ever induce him 'to set foot inside the thing'.

However, when one evening Allied bombers dropped marker flares over Saint-Germain, it seemed likely that bombs would follow. Zimmermann urged Leutnant Hans-Gerd von Rundstedt, the Field-Marshal's son who was acting as his father's aide-de-camp, to take him to the shelter. 'Young von Rundstedt succeeded eventually, and after meeting considerable opposition, in carrying out this order. As it happened the bombers hit a neighbouring suburb. I was much occupied on the telephone, and I forgot all about the Commander-in-Chief. An hour later my telephone rang. It was the Field-

After the meeting, the party had lunch in the garden. In this picture are (L-R) Oberst Bodo Zimmermann, the Ob. West Operations Officer; General der Infanterie Blumentritt; Generaloberst Guderian and Generalfeldmarschall von Rundstedt. (BA and ATB)

Marshal who simply asked, in his usual courteous fashion: "Zimmerman, can I please come out now?"'

Blumentritt: 'Matters were, of course, different for the Operations Staff of Ob. West. They had to be under strong concrete protection, with a complicated system of telephones, telegraphs, wireless stations, etc., so as to be able to carry on work in case matters became serious. Hence a large bunker was built for this working staff by the Organisation Todt about 300 metres from the villa.'

This huge bunker, built in an old quarry, measured about 60 metres long and provided about 40 rooms, not counting passages, corridors, and toilets.

Tired of active duty, the 69-year-old von Rundstedt was somewhat depressed at Saint-Germain and he found comfort in smoking a lot, and drinking too much (although no one reported him drunk). He was highly irritable and witnesses reported him throwing things to the ground in bursts of rage. To try to ease the atmosphere, Blumentritt (seen right posing in the garden of the Villa David) had the field-marshal's son, Hans-Gerd von Rundstedt, appointed to Saint-Germain as his father's aide-de-camp in early 1943. (BA)

A large brick building was erected nearby to provide additional office space. In addition, the Organisation Todt built air raid shelters near the buildings and villas occupied by the various Ob. West departments.

Resistance activities progressively increased in the region, the first skirmish between the Maquis and German troops taking place in the forest at Saint-Germain in March 1943. Then in August two

Oberst Zimmermann (left) and Leutnant von Rundstedt (right) seated with two other staff officers on the villa steps on the garden side. In 1945, Hans-Gerd was to follow his father into captivity in England but he soon fell ill with throat cancer and in mid-1947 had to be repatriated to Germany where he died the following January. (BA)

The I. Abteilung of the Heeresgruppen-Nachrichten-Regiment 570 provided communication for the Ob. West. Oberleutnant Robert Lanius addressed NCOs in the yard of the Gramont Barracks. (R. Lanius and ATB)

men fired at a German officer and sabotage was carried out at the major railway centre at nearby Achères. More sabotage at the Achères station took place in September; at the station at Saint-Germain in October, and again at Achères in November. As a result, stronger security measures were put in place around Ob. West, the whole headquarters area being cordoned off and the streets leading to it protected with rails planted in the ground and wire entanglements.

The telecommunication centre was installed in a requisitioned villa. Note the map showing the long-distance communication cables, with the hub in Paris at the bottom left. (R. Lanius)

The villa seems to have been demolished, replaced by apartment buildings, but this ordinary photo from Robert Lanius' album allows us to find the place where the I. Abteilung was once quartered. It was Rue de Tourville, opposite the intersection with Rue Molière. On April 18, 1941, the Heeresgruppen-Nachrichten-Regiment 570 secretly moved to the East to provide communication for the Heeresgruppe Süd. (R. Lanius and ATB)

FACING THE INVASION

EVER SINCE HIS RETURN to Ob. West in March 1942, von Rundstedt had sent report after report to the OKW pointing out the inadequacy of the preparations for the defence of France. In the spring of 1943, he personally visited Berchtesgaden to attempt to present his case to Hitler. It was some time after the fall of Stalingrad and the three-hour meeting consisted of a two-hour monologue by Hitler propounding his views on the Eastern Front.

In October 1943 he resumed his efforts and sent the OKW a comprehensive survey of the state of the defences in the West, requesting that it be brought to Hitler's personal attention. Hitler read the report with interest and on November 3 issued another basic order dealing with defence in the West: Führer Directive No. 51. Stipulating that there should be no more weakening of the West in favour of other theatres, he ordered those vulnerable portions of the coast be strengthened by the maximum emplacement of coastal artillery, anti-tank weapons, dug-in tanks, and mines. In addition, to counter any enemy breach of the coastal defences, the maximum mobile reserves should be assembled for a swift counter-attack.

Directive No. 51 marked a vigorous new beginning in the defence preparations in the West. Despite unforeseen emergencies on the Eastern Front and in Italy, between November 1943 and June 1944 the total number of divisions under Ob. West increased from 46 to 58. However, only ten of these were armoured or mechanised divisions.

In November 1943 Generalfeldmarschall Erwin Rommel entered the picture. Subordinated directly to the OKW, he was directed to inspect the coastal defences in the West and prepare operational studies for the employment of forces in defence and counter-attack. On December 19, Rommel had a first conference with the Ob. West staff in Paris. Oberst Zimmermann later recalled: 'Von Rundstedt outlined the situation briefly and sceptically, speaking of the poor quality of the troops, the dangerous weakness of the air force, the almost total absence of naval craft and stressing particularly the main defect of our defensive organisation, namely the complete lack of a powerful central reserve. He ended with the words: "It all looks very black to me". Afterwards the two field-marshals lunched together. A few senior staff officers, of whom I was one, were present. We expected one or other of the field-marshals to open the conversation, but neither showed any inclination to do so. Both were apparently preoccupied with their thoughts, which after their discussion can only have been of a most sombre hue. It was a strange, silent meal which will never be forgotten by any man who was present.'

As it was impractical for Rommel's special command to remain outside the

After his return to Ob. West in the spring of 1942, von Rundstedt repeatedly reported on the inadequacy of the defence preparations in the West. Meanwhile, German propaganda pictures conveyed an image of strength, like this one of a sentry overlooking the obstacle-packed beach at Étretat from a casemate armed with a 75mm gun. The casemate is no more but the view of the beach and its famous rocky outcrop, the Aiguille, remains the same.

Von Rundstedt's efforts finally paid off and in November 1943 Hitler issued Führer Directive No. 51, an order that marked a vigorous renewal of the defence preparations in the West. In the spring of 1943, von Rundstedt went to inspect the coastal defences, here in Blonville, south-west of Le Havre. The car, a Horch 930, displayed the command flag of an Army Group (on the front bumper) and the Field Marshal's command flag. (ATB and Google)

theatre chain of command, in late December von Rundstedt recommended that it be subordinated to Ob. West as Heeresgruppe B, with command of the 7. Armee and 15. Armee. This arrangement was adopted on January 15, 1944.

Rommel's experience in North Africa had convinced him of the folly of trying to move massed armour when the enemy enjoyed air superiority. He now stressed that the waters of the Channel and the strong points, entrenchments, mines, and wire of the Atlantic Wall offered the only means to defeat the Allies. He advocated that the battle would be decided at the

In the LXXXI. Armeekorps zone, on the left wing of the 15. Armee, Generalmajor Walther Leuze, commander of the fortified sector of Le Havre, explains the disposition of the defences to him. General der Panzertruppen Adolf Kuntzen, the commander of the LXXXI. Armeekorps, can be seen on the left and Generalmajor Herbert Olbrich, commanding the Luftwaffen-Feld-Division 17, in the centre background, between von Rundstedt and Leuze. (ECPAD)

Generalmajor Olbrich and one of his field commanders (this was the sector of the II. Bataillon of Luftwaffen-Jäger-Regiment 33) guiding von Rundstedt during inspection of what the Allies later designated Strongpoint No. 6 of the perimeter defence of Fortress Le Havre. These photos were taken at Fontaine-la-Mallet, just north of Le Havre, near the Ferme aux Cailloux. Several of the concrete positions inspected by von Rundstedt can still be seen today. (ECPAD)

Generalfeldmarschall Erwin Rommel entered the picture in November 1943. The following January, Rommel's command was named Heeresgruppe B and his headquarters was established in the château at La Roche-Guyon. Von Rundstedt and Rommel conferred several times during January and February to try to solve their basic disagreement on how best to meet the expected invasion. Here they are in the Grand Salon at La Roche-Guyon.

water's edge, and that the decisive phase would come within the first 48 hours of the landing. However, von Rundstedt and Rommel were in basic disagreement on how best to meet the expected invasion. Although they conferred several times during January and February, the conflict between their opposing beliefs between static or mobile defence was not resolved. Rommel's assumed authority and self-confidence, coupled with his favoured relationship with Hitler, placed him in a position to challenge von Rundstedt. Consequently, the defence preparations in the West were constantly scarred by compromise, both field-marshals making decisions in accordance with their divergent aims.

In March 1944, Rommel asked for his own remit to be extended, requesting that all armoured units in the West be put under his direct command. As von Rundstedt's protest was supported by the OKW, Hitler only partly agreed to Rommel's demand. Three panzer divisions were assigned to Heeresgruppe B as reserves while four others – three panzer and one panzergrenadier – were set aside as a central mobile reserve under the direct command of the OKW. Rommel soon moved one of the reserve divisions allocated to him, the 21. Panzer-Division, closer to the coast along both sides of the Orne River in Normandy, and in May he requested that the four panzer divisions in OKW reserve be also moved nearer to the coast. When von Rundstedt protested, pointing out that such a move committed the units before the location of the landings was known, Rommel's demand was turned down.

At the beginning of June 1944, the command in the West was organised as follows:

Ob. West, Generalfeldmarschall von Rundstedt, headquarters in Saint-Germain-en-Laye, controlled two army groups, Heeresgruppe B under Generalfeldmarschall Rommel and Armeegruppe G under Generaloberst Johannes Blaskowitz. The boundary between the two army groups was an east-

Generalleutnant Hans Speidel (Chief-of-Staff of Heeresgruppe B from mid-April 1944), Rommel, Guderian and General der Panzertruppen Leo Geyr von Schweppenburg (commander of Panzergruppe West) during one of these difficult conferences, the one held in the Grand Salon at La Roche-Guyon on April 28. At this meeting, as Guderian later reported, Rommel turned down all his suggestions, backing his 'highly temperamental and strongly expressed refusal' with the remark that Guderian was 'a man from the Eastern Front' lacking experience of the Western enemy armies.

The château of La Roche-Guyon was opened to the public in 1994, and the Grand Salon, located in the part of the building known as the Corps de Logis which dates back to the 16th century, is one of the rooms that can be visited.

west line across France from the Loire estuary to Geneva. North of this line lay Heeresgruppe B with headquarters in La Roche-Guyon. The army group controlled the LXXXVIII. Armeekorps which occupied the Netherlands; the 15. Armee of Generaloberst Hans von Salmuth (headquarters in Tourcoing) which defended the Channel coast from Antwerp to the Orne River, and the

Then and Now at La Roche-Guyon. The picture above was taken in the spring of 1944 when Generalmajor Walter Botsch, the Chief-of-Staff of the 19. Armee (centre), visited Heeresgruppe B headquarters. (ECPAD)

The château owner, the Count De la Rochefoucauld, (not seen in this German photo of Generalmajor Botsch) continued to live there the during the time that it was requisitioned for Rommel's headquarters.

Most of the Ob. West staff moved to hotels in Paris during the winter months, particularly to the Hôtel George V. This hotel and the one next door, the Prince de Galles, also served as convenient locations for major meetings or conferences, even in the summer months. (BA and ATB)

7. Armee of Generaloberst Friedrich Dollmann (headquarters in Le Mans) which held north-west France between the Orne and the Loire rivers.

South of the boundary was the territory of Armeegruppe G with headquarters in Toulouse, which commanded the 1. Armee of General Joachim Lemelsen (HQ in Bordeaux), defending the French Atlantic coast from the Loire to the Spanish border, and the 19. Armee of General Georg von Sodenstern (HQ in Avignon), responsible for the Mediterranean coast of France.

On June 5, von Rundstedt reported: 'it is still obscure where the enemy will attempt a landing' and concluded: 'as yet there is no immediate prospect of the invasion'. Rommel was equally confident and left France for Germany by car early on June 5, intending to drive to his home at Herrlingen to celebrate his wife's birthday on the 6th, and then to visit Hitler at Berchtesgaden on the 8th.

The Avenue George V, looking southwards, showing the close relationship between the two hotels. They still rank among the most prominent in Paris, having received numerous world leaders and hosted many more conferences since the days of Ob. West. (BA and ATB)

On May 8, 1944, von Rundstedt called for a top-level conference at the Prince de Galles to settle the strategic issue. (BA)

Generaloberst Johannes Blaskowitz, the commander of Armeegruppe G, arrives at the meeting. The Avenue George V, looking north from the entrance to the Prince de Galles. (BA and ATB)

Before the meeting in the Prince de Galles' basement suite, now the Salon Ascot, Admiral Theodor Krancke, commander of Marinegruppe West (left) chats with Generalfeldmarschall Hugo Sperrle, commander of Luftflotte 3 (right), and three chiefs-of-staff: Generalleutnant Speidel, Chief-of-Staff of Heeresgruppe B, General der Infanterie Blumentritt, Chief-of-Staff of Ob. West, and Generalmajor Hermann Plocher, Chief-of-Staff of Luftflotte 3. (BA)

The meeting convened under the chairmanship of von Rundstedt. L-R: General der Panzertruppen Geyr von Schweppenburg, Generaloberst Blaskowitz, Generalfeldmarschall Sperrle, von Rundstedt, Rommel, and Admiral Krancke. Across the table in front of them were their respective chiefs-of-staff. General der Infanterie Blumentritt, Generalleutnant Speidel and Generalmajor Plocher. (BA)

Before getting down to business, the generals gave Kriegsberichter Jesse time to take a few pictures.

Salon Ascot Then and Now. In the spring of 2008, *After the Battle* had the exceptional opportunity to make this remarkable comparison.

D-DAY

OBERST ZIMMERMANN, Ob. West Operations Officer: 'At about a quarter past nine in the evening of June 5, I was in our officer's mess at Saint-Germain when the chief intelligence officer of the staff of Ob. West [Oberstleutnant Wilhelm Meyer-Detring] came to look for me. He was in a state of high excitement, for his people had just decoded a British wireless message. It was the habit of the Allies to communicate with their many agents in the West by radio, and not infrequently our experts succeeded in decoding these apparently harmless signals. This, however, was a signal of a very different type, for it ordered the mobilisation of the entire French resistance movement for the coming night. This could have only one meaning: the invasion was about to begin.'

There followed a 'telegraphic blitz' on all command and control centres in the West. The 15. Armee ordered a general alert and the 7. Armee followed

It appears that no photos were taken at Ob. West in Saint-Germain on June 6, 1944 – D-Day. However, a sequence from the 1962 war film *The Longest Day* provides a genuine substitute. The sequence begins about six minutes from the start of the movie and first shows Oberstleutnant Hellmuth Meyer (played by Heinz Spitzner), the 15. Armee Intelligence Officer, receiving the first half of the Chanson d'Automne poem by Verlaine and wondering when the second part is to come. The poem was a coded message to the French resistance to alert them for the upcoming invasion. If German intelligence was correct, on receipt of the second part, the invasion would begin within the next 48 hours. The poem's second half was recorded at Tourcoing at 9.15 p.m. on June 5 and Ob. West at Saint-Germain was immediately warned. (*The Longest Day*)

The movie then shows Blumentritt coming to see von Rundstedt at his villa. The scene of Blumentritt arriving by car was shot at Saint-Germain, in the yard of what was then the Lycée de Jeunes Filles. The bunker seen in the left background was a mock-up, but genuine wartime bunkers were still standing, as they are today, a few metres away on either side of the cameraman.
(*The Longest Day*)

suit although many of its senior officers could not be contacted as they were en route returning from a conference that had been held at Rennes. Shortly after midnight, von Rundstedt alerted the 12. SS-Panzer-Division and the Panzer-Lehr-Division, two of the divisions in the mobile reserve under command of the OKW, who were informed of the measures taken.

Zimmermann: 'All this was done quite quickly. And then, for a time, nothing more happened. Midnight passed, one o'clock, and still no further messages reached Saint-Germain. At about two o'clock we were ready to believe that it was just another false alarm, when Heeresgruppe B rang through, reporting parachute landings in Normandy shortly after midnight.'

From the location of the airborne forces, Ob. West calculated that a seaborne assault would follow at first light between the Cotentin peninsula and the Orne River. About 3 a.m., without waiting for approval from the OKW, von Rundstedt ordered the 12. SS-Panzer-Division to move as quickly as possible to Lisieux and the Panzer-Lehr-Division to Albert whereupon

The scene was not filmed at von Rundstedt's real quarters, the Villa David, but at a nearby villa that had also been used by Ob. West. Some sources claim that it had been Blumentritt's quarters, which may have some credibility as Blumentritt himself had been one of the military consultants to the movie production team. (*The Longest Day*)

both would come under command of Heeresgruppe B. The OKW responded some time after six o'clock.

Zimmermann: 'In violent terms von Rundstedt was upbraided for his orders to the two panzer divisions which, we were informed, should not have been moved without the prior approval of the OKW. One cannot yet say for sure where the main invasion will come and, besides, Hitler has not yet decided.'

When Generalfeldmarschall Wilhelm Keitel, the chief of the OKW, and Generaloberst Alfred Jodl, the head of the OKW Operations Staff, came to see him about 8 a.m., Hitler greeted them with the words: 'Meine Herren, this is the invasion'. However, it was not before the usual conference held that afternoon that the commitment of the two panzer divisions by Ob. West was considered and finally approved. Harassed from the air, the two divisions were much delayed and suffered losses trying to reach their destinations. Their counter-attacks were not launched until June 7 and 8 and achieved nothing. On June 9 Heeresgruppe B had to turn to the defensive.

On June 11, von Rundstedt and Rommel met to discuss the very serious situation and agreed that they would report independently to Hitler. Von

Blumentritt (played by Curt Jürgens) proposed to von Rundstedt (Paul Hartmann, a good look-alike, albeit a little too heavyweight) to sound the general alert in the West. Von Rundstedt was sceptical that there was any truth in such coded messages as he did not believe that the enemy would risk warning that they were coming just to get some Resistance fighters active. He insisted that too many alerts were already affecting discipline and moral. 'No, Blumentritt. No alert!' The time was about 10 p.m. and von Rundstedt was in dressing gown . . . but in the film we have seen Blumentritt's car arriving in full daylight! (*The Longest Day*)

The scene was shot on the first floor of the villa. The elaborate wall decoration has been removed but the angled part of the wall and the window remain to establish the location. This building is today part of the Lycée Jeanne d'Albret and we are indebted to its director when we inquired in 1993, Madame Zanaret, for allowing us access to the school.

Rundstedt's memorandum was sent to the OKW the same day, Rommel's one day later. While both reports gave the same appreciation of the German situation and of the Allies' intentions, von Rundstedt pointed out that offensive operations could not yet be conducted in the sector between the Orne and the Vire 'for lack of forces and because the panzer divisions had to be used for defence'. He stated that the troops were fighting well, that morale was good, but warned that 'the material superiority of the Anglo-Americans must in the long run have its effect on any troops'. To prevent a breakthrough to Cherbourg, which was seen as the immediate American objective, he and Rommel proposed to counter-attack in the Cotentin.

Hitler's reaction on June 11 was to order the transfer of the II. SS-

Von Rundstedt was relieved of his command at the beginning of July and Generalfeldmarschall Günther von Kluge then assumed command of Ob. West. (BA)

Panzerkorps, comprising the 9. and 10. SS-Panzer-Divisions, from the East. However, he showed no true appreciation of the vital need for immediate action in Normandy and on the 12th, refusing the field-marshals' demand for a counter-attack in the Cotentin, insisted that 'the enemy bridgehead between the Orne and the Vire must be attacked and destroyed piece by piece'.

Worried that Hitler and his staff obviously failed to understand the true situation in Normandy, on the 15th von Rundstedt asked that either Generaloberst Jodl or General der Artillerie Walter Warlimont (Jodl's deputy) should come to France to discuss the situation and report back to Hitler. Instead, Hitler decided to come personally and a conference was arranged at a complex of camouflaged bunkers at Margival, 15 kilometres north-east of Soissons. Code-named Wolfsschlucht 2, this Führerhauptquartier had been prepared in 1943-44 for Hitler to personally direct the defence when the expected invasion came. From Berchtesgaden, Hitler was flown to France on the evening of June 16 with Jodl and a few officers of the OKW Operations Staff. Landing at Metz, the party was driven to Margival early next morning. Von Rundstedt and Rommel arrived with their Chiefs-of-Staff and some subordinate officers.

The conference started at 9.30 a.m. in a large meeting room in a bunker. Rommel's Chief-of-Staff, Generalleutnant Hans Speidel, in his book Invasion 1944 (published in 1949) described how 'Hitler looked pale and sleepless.

Another set of photos shows the field-marshal receiving what appears to be a party from Berlin. On July 17, Rommel was seriously injured when Allied aircraft strafed his car in Normandy and OKW then informed von Kluge that he would have to command Heeresgruppe B in addition to his own responsibility as Ob. West. As a result, von Kluge moved to Rommel's headquarters at La Roche-Guyon while Blumentritt remained at Saint-Germain in his absence. (BA)

Having tracked down this new series of photos, I returned to Villa David only to find that this corner of the room where the party had gathered, then offices at the Collège Marcel Roby, was cluttered with cupboards. However, M. René Bonnet, the then school director, quickly called for help and in a few minutes the spot was cleared.

A perfect comparison of von Kluge reassuring the visitors from Berlin. Over six decades later, the wall panelling and radiator remained the same. (BA and ATB)

Nervously he played with his spectacles and an array of coloured pencils which he held between his fingers . . . His old personal magnetism seemed to have gone. After brief and cool greetings, Hitler, raising his voice, first expressed sharp dissatisfaction with the successful Allied landings, found fault with the local commanders, and then ordered that Festung Cherbourg be held at any cost.'

Von Rundstedt requested that he be given a strategic instruction for the conduct of the war in the West 'to make freedom of action possible'. Blumentritt recalled: 'Contrarily to expectation, this request was received calmly and an instruction was actually promised'. Rommel begged leave to withdraw to shorten the lines and mass forces for a major counter-attack but this request was refused. Hitler soon changed the subject, showing off pictures of new aircraft and talking of the effects of the V-weapon attacks. 'The impression arose', wrote Blumentritt, 'that Hitler diverted himself by this means from the bitter knowledge of the real situation'.

The conference ended just after midday with no relaxation of the order to hold every position everywhere, denying the western commanders freedom of action. During the meal that followed in a small wooden chalet, Hitler spoke to the two sullen field-marshals. Later, when the conference reconvened, Rommel again tried to make Hitler realise the gravity of the situation and he even dared to suggest that it was time to come to terms with the Western Allies. Jodl later recalled how Hitler retorted sharply: 'That is a question which is not your responsibility. You will have to leave that to me'. (Speidel in his memoirs places this incident inside the air raid shelter, see below).

At around 3 p.m., an air raid warning was sounded and Hitler took the two field-marshals and their Chiefs-of-Staff into an air raid shelter. They remained there for about an hour, hardly a word being spoken. Shortly after the two field-marshals had departed, a defective V-1 exploded about two kilometres from the Führerhauptquartier. Although it caused no casualties, the incident alarmed Hitler and his staff and they left in the evening, cancelling a new meeting agreed for June 19 at Rommel's headquarters at La Roche-Guyon.

On June 20, the OKW confirmed the terms of the major counter-attack which had been discussed at Margival. It was to split the Allies on the coast and then dispose of each of them separately. On June 21, Heeresgruppe B issued the operational plan. There would be a delay of 10-14 days as only two of the six armoured divisions – the Panzer-Lehr-Division and the 2. Panzer-Division – were in place. A third, the 2. SS-Panzer-Division, was beginning to assemble near Saint-Lô but air attacks had caused much hindrance and its last elements did not reach the battle area until June 23. The other three divisions were also still en route: the 1. SS-Panzer-Division from Belgium and the 9. and 10. SS-Panzer-Divisions from the East.

On June 26 von Rundstedt and Rommel were summoned to Berchtesgaden. To minimise the risk, they were not allowed to fly or travel by train so they went separately by road, an exhausting drive of about 20 hours. The meeting on the evening of June 29 lasted about three hours. The field-marshals were tired and on edge as Hitler enunciated his strategy. He would not hear of any withdrawal or any tactical adjustments of the lines and simply restated his stand-at-all-cost tactics. Later that night, after von Rundstedt and Rommel had already started on the long journey back, the OKW issued orders confirming Hitler's strategy.

Returning to Saint-Germain on the evening of June 30, von Rundstedt found the new OKW directive waiting for him. Later that evening he lost temper during a telephone conversation with Keitel. When asked what they should do, von Rundstedt is reputed to have retorted: 'Make peace, you fools. What else can we do?'

With Hitler's patience at breaking point, he decided to relieve von Rundstedt of his command on grounds of age and health, and on July 2 he sent his adjutant, Oberstleutnant Heinrich Borgmann, to present von Rundstedt with the Oak Leaves to his Knight's Cross. (Although von Rundstedt later

Exchange of Nazi salutes as the delegation from Berlin left. Von Kluge and his collaborators relax in front of the villa. (BA and ATB)

denied ever having expressed his desire to retire, the Ob. West war diaries state that he did so, which was also confirmed by Blumentritt.)

The following morning Generalfeldmarschall Günther von Kluge arrived at Saint-Germain to assume command of Ob. West. According to Speidel (in his book Invasion 1944), the briefing which von Kluge had received from Hitler and Jodl before taking over 'had convinced him that the events in the West were the result of mistakes and omissions on the part of the commanders and troops'. When he arrived at the headquarters, von Kluge seemed to Blumentritt to be 'cheerful and confident . . . almost gay about the prospects'.

However, it was a grim situation that von Kluge inherited. In a report written on July 15, Rommel had stressed that the losses had been 'so great that the fighting strength of our divisions is sinking rapidly' and pointed out that while his army group had lost 97,000 casualties since the beginning of the invasion, he had received just 10,000 replacements, of whom only about 6,000 had yet reached the front. Material losses too had been high and had so far been replaced only on a very small scale: for example, some 225 tanks had been lost but only 17 replacements had arrived.

COMMAND CRISIS

ON THE AFTERNOON OF JULY 17 Rommel was on his way back from the headquarters of I. SS-Panzerkorps when aircraft strafed his car. Fatally wounded, the driver lost control and Rommel was hurled on to the road and badly injured. Two days later OKW advised von Kluge that, as no suitable replacement for Rommel was available, he would have to command Heeresgruppe B in addition to his own responsibility as Ob. West. As a result, von Kluge moved to Rommel's headquarters at La Roche-Guyon while Blumentritt remained back at Saint-Germain in his absence.

On July 20, as von Kluge was at the front conferring with his senior commanders, over a thousand kilometres away at Rastenburg in East Prussia Hitler narrowly escaped an attempt on his life when the bomb placed in the conference room of the Führerhauptquartier by Oberst Claus Schenk von Stauffenberg exploded at 12.42 p.m. In Paris, those officers who were members of the conspiracy received the pre-arranged code-word from their opposite numbers in Berlin at 2.30 p.m. signalling that the operation to kill Hitler had been successful. On receipt of the word 'Abgelaufen', the Military Governor of France, General Carl-Heinrich von Stülpnagel, acted with dispatch. Telephone lines with Berlin were cut and measures were taken to arrest all personnel belonging to the SS and SD security services in Paris.

Von Kluge was ignorant of these developments until he returned to La Roche-Guyon at about six o'clock that evening. Speidel appraised him of events and showed him two messages which had been received. The first, telephoned by Blumentritt, said that Hitler was dead and that a revolt had broken out in Berlin. The second, received some time later, was from a broadcast and stated that the attempt to kill Hitler had failed.

At 7 p.m. von Kluge was telephoned from Berlin by the conspirators. The caller gave no name (he was, it is believed, General Ludwig Beck) but he confirmed that Hitler was dead and urged him to act at once. The confusion continued when at 7.28 p.m. an order signed by the new Commander-in-Chief of the Wehrmacht, Generalfeldmarschall Erwin von Witzleben, arrived. This made quite an impression on von Kluge until a telex signed by Keitel at 8 p.m. stated that any orders signed by von Witzleben were not valid.

Half an hour earlier, von Stülpnagel had arrived at La Roche-Guyon with an officer from his staff, Oberstleutnant Cäsar von Hofacker, who was one of the main conspirators in the West. They spent the whole evening trying to persuade von Kluge to lead the revolt on the Western Front whether Hitler was dead or not but, according to Blumentritt, von Kluge 'with obvious disappointment' concluded: 'Well, gentlemen, the attempt has failed. Everything is over'. At the dinner table, in a final attempt to commit him, von

On August 15 von Kluge got lost all day on his way to a front meeting with his generals (Allied planes strafed his party and destroyed his radio car). Hitler then became convinced that this absence was due to the fact that von Kluge had tried to contact the Allies to arrange the surrender of the German forces in the West and decided to remove him. This photo of von Kluge and General Eberbach, commander of the 5. Panzerarmee, was taken a few weeks earlier at Eberbach's headquarters south of Caen.

Stülpnagel told von Kluge about the measures he had already taken in Paris (it was around 10 p.m.). He said that the Nazi administrators and Gestapo – a total of about 1,200 men – would by now have been arrested. Unrelenting, von Kluge ordered von Stülpnagel to return to Paris with instructions to undo what he had done.

In the early hours of the 21st, Blumentritt telephoned from Saint-Germain to advise that von Stülpnagel should be suspended and von Kluge agreed. Blumentritt also suggested that Ob. West should send a letter of congratulations and loyalty to Hitler. Praising the 'gracious dispensation of Providence' which had saved the Führer's life from 'ruthless murderers', von Kluge concluded, 'in the name of the three services subordinate to me as Ob. West, we congratulate you and assure you, my Führer, of our unchangeable loyalty, come what may'. Then, just before 1 p.m., Hitler made an all-station broadcast so that the German people 'should hear my voice and should know that I am unhurt and well'.

The round-up then began. Summoned to report to Keitel, von Stülpnagel attempted suicide on his way to Germany but failed to die. He was taken to hospital, tried by the People's Court, and hanged one month later. Many others paid with their lives for their part in the attempted coup d'état, among them Generalfeldmarschall von Witzleben. Rommel, recuperating at home from his injury, was eventually forced to commit suicide and his former Chief-of-Staff, Speidel, and even von Kluge were soon to fall under suspicion.

Meanwhile the situation on the front was so grave that von Kluge chose this most inappropriate time to write a long memorandum to Hitler. 'In spite of intense efforts, the moment is fast approaching when our hard-pressed defences will break. Once the enemy has erupted into open country, the inadequate mobility of our forces will make orderly and effective conduct of the battle hardly possible. I consider it my duty as the commander responsible for this front to bring these conclusions to your notice, my Führer, in good time.'

With no respite, on July 25 the Allies launched Operation 'Cobra', the Americans soon breached the German front in the Cotentin, and by the end of the month they had broken out at Avranches. When Blumentritt telephoned on the 31st that OKW was asking about the locations of the rearward defences, von Kluge could not hide his derision. 'All you can do is laugh out loud. Don't they read our dispatches? Haven't they been oriented? They must be living on the moon.'

Far divorced from the realities of the battle in the West, Hitler now decided to launch a major counter-attack to regain control of the situation in Normandy. Code-named Operation 'Lüttich', the strong armoured strike toward Mortain began on August 6 but it soon exhausted itself, having achieved nothing yet Hitler insisted that it should be renewed.

Early on the morning of August 15 von Kluge was driving to Nécy, ten kilometres south of Falaise, for a meeting with his senior commanders when his party was subjected to an air attack which knocked out his radio car. Consequently, he vanished from view for most of the day, only turning up at Panzergruppe Eberbach's headquarters after dark in a very shaken condition.

Having returned to 5. Panzerarmee's headquarters at Meulles where communications were better, at 2 a.m. on August 16 von Kluge despatched a decisive report to Jodl. He stated that the forces available were not strong enough and that he had insufficient fuel supplies to launch a counter-stroke of decisive value. He said that the troops in the western salient must withdraw immediately through the Falaise-Argentan gap and he warned that any delay in accepting his recommendation would result in 'unforeseeable developments'.

That afternoon Hitler finally issued orders which marked an admission that his armies in the West had been defeated. At 4.45 p.m. on August 16, Ob. West received the order permitting the withdrawal of those forces that were west of the Argentan gap, first behind the Orne and then behind the Dives. The directive emphasised two points: 'Falaise will be held tenaciously as a bastion' and that the Argentan-Falaise gap had to be enlarged by armoured attacks south-eastward.

As Hitler was blaming von Kluge for what he perceived as the mismanagement of Operation 'Lüttich', rumours – totally unfounded – began to circulate that the latter's absence on the 15th could have been because he had been trying to contact the Allies to arrange the surrender of the German forces in the West. Hitler already had doubts about von Kluge's loyalty after what had happened in Paris on July 20, and he now convinced himself that von Kluge had 'planned to lead the whole of the western army to capitulation'. He therefore decided to remove him. Early on August 16, he summoned Generalfeldmarschall Walter Model, then commanding Heeresgruppe Nordukraine on the Eastern Front, and Jodl gave Model verbal directives on the future conduct of the operations in the West, particularly for the establishment of a new front on the line of the Seine and Yonne rivers.

That same day von Kluge held a conference at Saint-Germain with Generalfeldmarschall Hugo Sperrle and Admiral Theodor Krancke, the Commanders-in-Chief of the Luftwaffe and the Kriegsmarine in the West, and Generalleutnant Dietrich von Choltitz, the Military Commander of Greater Paris.

Early on August 16, Generalfeldmarschall Walter Model, then commanding Heeresgruppe Nordukraine on the Eastern Front, was summoned to replace von Kluge. Model arrived on the night of the 17th, and von Kluge left on the morning of the 18th. Two days later, near Metz, while on his way to Germany by car, he ordered the driver to stop and he took poison. He was buried in Böhne in Kreis Rathenau, without public ceremony.

Commenting on the meeting, Zimmermann pondered: 'Did he know that his fate was already decided? It was noticed that he said good-bye to each officer personally, and there was something melancholy in his manner of doing so. Then he returned to La Roche-Guyon, where Field-Marshal Model arrived during the night of the 17th, bearing with him the order whereby he was to supersede von Kluge as Ob. West and as commander of Heeresgruppe B. He also brought von Kluge a short letter from Hitler, in which Hitler said that von Kluge had overtired himself during the weeks of battle and that Hitler had therefore decided to transfer him to the army reserve pool for a period of recuperation. Von Kluge took his dismissal quite calmly. That night he wrote a letter to Hitler imploring him to end the unequal battle in the West. Early on the 18th he said good-bye to his staff officers and set out by car for Germany.'

In his personal letter to Hitler, von Kluge justified his conduct of operations and declared his loyalty. 'If Fate is stronger than your will and your genius, that is Destiny. You have made an honourable and tremendous fight. History will testify for you. Show now that greatness that will be necessary if it comes to the point of ending a struggle which has become hopeless.' Two days later near Metz, while on his way to Germany by car, von Kluge ordered the driver to pull over. He took poison and was driven to Met

WITHDRAWAL FROM FRANCE

AT THE SAME TIME that he had ordered the Mortain counter-attack, Hitler had had to consider the eventuality of withdrawing from Normandy, perhaps from the whole of France. To cover the withdrawal, the OKW on August 2 ordered General Kitzinger, Military Governor of France, to organise defensive positions along the line of the Somme, Marne and Saône rivers, to which the forces fighting in Normandy would retire. As far as Paris was concerned, the German high command felt that its loss to the Allies would publicise the extent of the German reverses, and thus decided the French capital must

From mid-August, the German forces in Normandy retreated rapidly, day and night. Kriegsberichter Kurth photographed a Sturmgeschütz rattling up Rue de la République in Orbec, the Seine was still 60 kilometres away. (ECPAD)

In Brionne, Rue du Maréchal Foch, Kurth photographed this SdKfz 250 light armoured vehicle. The Seine was still more than 30 kilometres away. (ECPAD)

be held. On August 7 Generalleutnant von Choltitz was appointed Military Commander of Greater Paris.

His predecessor, Generalleutnant Hans von Boineburg-Lengsfeld, had already started the construction of a defensive line west and south-west of Paris as he believed that fighting inside the city would be an act of complete irresponsibility because of the almost certain destruction of irreplaceable art treasures. Elements of the 325. Sicherungs-Division, the security division in charge of the French capital since 1942, and anti-aircraft units soon occupied these positions to block the main highway approaches to the capital.

With the appointment of von Choltitz, more forces were deployed west and south-west of Paris, and an anti-tank expert, Oberst Hermann Oehmichen, arrived from Germany to instruct local units the techniques of opposing armour. Von Kluge had placed Generalmajor Hubertus von Aulock in command of the perimeter defence west and south-west of Paris. (To face the gravity of the situation, von Aulock was promoted on the spot from Oberstleutnant to the rank of Generalmajor.) By mid-August this sector was manned by about 20,000 men, though neither of high quality nor experienced in combat.

Still at Brionne, Kurth took this photograph of two Jagdpanthers of the schwere Panzerjäger-Abteilung 654, the leader having the other in tow. (ECPAD)

All the bridges on the Seine below Paris were destroyed, and German engineers worked frantically to build emergency crossings across the river. They succeeded and ultimately operated 60 ferry and boat crossings as well as three pontoon bridges during the last days of August. In Caudebec-en-Caux, downstream from Rouen, engineers improvised this pontoon using two inflatable boats tied on each side of a motorised boat. This improvised pontoon could transport a light vehicle. (ECPAD)

Just upstream Rouen, the Eauplet railway bridge was destroyed by an Allied air attack in May and the German engineers achieved a patchy repair which made the bridge usable for vehicles. Kriegsberichter Karl Müller photographed these men leaning a hand for this lorry to climb up the steep patched bridge. (ECPAD)

In Caudebec-les-Elbeuf, upstream of Rouen, Kriegsberichter Hans Scheck photographed a small ferry in operation. It could carry up to three tonnes. (ECPAD)

From August 20, bad weather prevented Allied air intervention and gave the Germans four days of respite. Conditions improved on the 25th and that evening, 24 Mitchells and 10 Bostons from the Nos 137 and 139 Wings bombarded the traffic jam of hundreds of vehicles waiting to cross on the west bank of the Seine at Rouen. From the east bank, while the west bank was an inferno of flames, Kriegsberichter Jesse photographed a ferry hastily docking and the men on board running for cover. (ECPAD)

Investigation later revealed a total of 680 wrecks, including 20 armoured vehicles and 48 guns, in this area of the west bank of the Seine.

On August 28, Model issued instructions for the defence of the Somme. With scattered staffs, virtually non-existent communications, and congested roads, the German command had great difficulty maintaining any semblance of order during the withdrawal to the Somme. On August 14, M. Watteeuw, a local photographer, took this remarkable photo of Tiger '113' in Beauvais. It was one of 14 Tiger IIs of the 1. Kompanie of the schwere SS-Panzer-Abteilung 101 that were moving to man the intermediate defensive positions between the Seine and the Somme. (F. Watteeuw)

At Saint-Germain, the evacuation of the Ob. West headquarters personnel had begun at the beginning of August, and by the 10th all the female staff had left. Stocks of supplies were withdrawn, the evacuation accelerated, and most of the buildings and villas were soon empty. Traffic signs pointing the direction of Metz and Cologne, far away to the east, appeared on August 14 and movements of withdrawing troops increased.

Oberst Kurt Hesse, the commander of the local Feldkommandantur 758, was organising the defence of the Versailles–Saint-Germain sector, deploying the scratch elements sent to him, among which was a battalion from Sicherungs-Regiment 66. On the 17th he ordered that all men between 18 to 50 years of age living in Saint-Germain were to assemble next morning in front of the Château to build obstacles in the city streets but the only person who turned up was the Mayor! Resorting to press-gang tactics to recruit more labour, the Organisation Todt issued personal summons to qualified persons ordering them to report for work on the morning of the 20th. Conscripts turned up as summoned but an altercation led to a Todt officer opening fire, killing one woman in front of the church, and badly wounding two others.

On August 19, American forces crossed the Seine near Mantes, forcing

Lead units of the US XV Corps reached the Seine near Mantes, downstream of Paris, on August 18 and crossed the river on the 20th. Relaxed GIs stands at the west end of the destroyed bridge. (USNA)

The 5th Infantry Division leading the American XX Corps reached the Seine near Fontainebleau, upstream from Paris, on August 23. This photo was taken one kilometre from the site near Samoreau where a pontoon bridge was soon to be built. (USNA)

Heeresgruppe B headquarters to withdraw from La Roche-Guyon. The staff pulled out under American artillery fire and re-established themselves in the Führerhauptquartier 'Wolfsschlucht 2' installations at Margival. In the meantime, Ob. West headquarters vacated Saint-Germain to become operational again on the 20th at Verzy near Reims. Model and his Heeresgruppe B headquarters left Margival on the 28th, having been operational there for just ten days, to establish in the château at Havrincourt, near Cambrai. By then, the Ob. West staff was on its way to Germany.

At Saint-Germain, as more withdrawing troops crossed the city, and stray individuals commandeered every means of transport, including bicycles, three Panther tanks took up positions near the Place Royale. Large explosions could be heard from the 21st onwards as the Germans started to destroy remaining equipment and stores.

At dawn on the 24th, the French 2ème Division Blindée drove on Paris from the south. Having broken through the German defence line, shortly before midnight its lead elements reached the Hôtel de Ville. The German defences to the west and south-west that had held out during the day melted away during the night after von Choltitz had ordered von Aulock to withdraw behind the Seine.

The pontoon bridge was opened to traffic on the evening of the 24th, and the original caption for this photo indicates that it was taken when the first tank rolled over. The fact that there is not a single wheel or track mark on the east bank in the foreground proves that this was indeed the first vehicle to cross. (USNA)

Downstream from Mantes, the British XXX Corps reached the Seine at Vernon on the 24th and the next day the 129th Brigade of the 43rd (Wessex) Division forced the crossing. (SSETO)

At Saint-Germain, the final evacuation took place on the 24th, explosions continuing during the night, and by 4 a.m. on the 25th the last Germans had gone. That morning, the Resistance occupied the Gramont barracks near the Place Royale and the French tricolour appeared on the Town Hall and numerous other houses and buildings. At around 7 p.m. a single American Jeep arrived carrying Captains Mark Lillard and Jack Weber of the US 5th Armored Division who found Saint-Germain devoid of any Germans. An hour or so later a massive explosion rent the air as German engineers blew the Seine bridge at Le Pecq. Saint-Germain-en-Laye was finally liberated on August 26 when American tanks entered the city cheered by a madly joyful population.

Model and the staff of Heeresgruppe B withdrew from La Roche-Guyon on August 19, under American artillery fire, and settled in the installations of the Führerhauptquartier 'W2' in Margival. In the meantime, Ob. West headquarters vacated Saint-Germain to become operational again on the 20th at Verzy near Reims. Model and his Heeresgruppe B headquarters left Margival on the 28th, having been operational there for ten days, to establish in the château at Havrincourt, near Cambrai. By then, the Ob. West staff was on its way to Germany. It does not appear that any photographs were taken of Model at Havrincourt in August or September 1944 but we traced pictures of von Kluge, his predecessor at Ob. West, in the same château. That was in 1940 when von Kluge commanded the 4. Armee.

At Saint-Germain, from mid-August, on orders from Oberst Kurt Hesse, anti-tank barriers began to be built in the streets, the Organisation Todt soon resorting to forcefully rounding up civilians to do the job. Through the slatted shutters of his flat, Maurice Veillon discreetly photographed conscripts erecting obstacles in the Rue du Vieil Abreuvoir. The château can be seen in the background. (M. Veillon)

There was no battle in Saint-Germain, however, for during the night of August 24/25 Generalleutnant von Choltitz ordered the troops defending outer Paris to withdraw behind the Seine. A motley battle group, Kampfgruppe Pulkowski, retreated via Saint-Germain, Argenteuil and Sarcelles. The battle group commander, Hauptmann Ferdinand Pulkowski later recounted: 'It is starting to get light, the streets are deserted. Sometimes, windows open as we approach and flowers are thrown to us. Understanding their mistake, the inhabitants look as if frozen in fear from the top of their windows, then quickly close them. They were waiting for the Americans, not us!' In the Kampfgruppe was a handful of tanks, Panthers and PzKpfw IVs, under the command of an SS-Hauptsturmführer Schwieckart, possibly from the 17. SS-Panzergrenadier-Division. Discreetly taken photos of three of these Panthers, one of them in tow, heading east on rue Édouard Vaillant in Bezons, 10 kilometres east of Saint-Germain. Things soon took a turn for the worse when the FFIs attacked the column at Saint-Denis, then at Sarcelles, and the Germans had to fight their way out, not without losses. (Bruno Renoult)

On the night of August 24, leading elements of the 2ème Division Blindée entered Paris and reached the City Hall shortly before midnight. The next morning, the remainder of the division and the US 4th Infantry Division entered the city. This photo taken on the 25th shows elements of the 2ème Division Blindée advancing on Avenue de l'Opéra. (SSETO)

Breaking through a barricade in Rue de Rivoli, 'Douaumont', a Sherman of the 2ème Division Blindée, entered the Place de la Concorde a few ten metres from a Panther then exchanging shots with other Shermans on the Avenue des Champs Élysées. 'Douaumont' fired HE shells at the Panther, to no effect, and the crew commander, Sergent Marcel Bizien, then directed his driver to ram the German tank. Its turret jammed, the German crew bailed out and ran away.

In the evening of August 25, General Dietrich von Choltitz, the commander of Greater Paris, signed a formal act of capitulation.

The Germans finally evacuated Saint-Germain on August 24 and by next morning the French tricolour was flying on the Town Hall and numerous houses in the city.

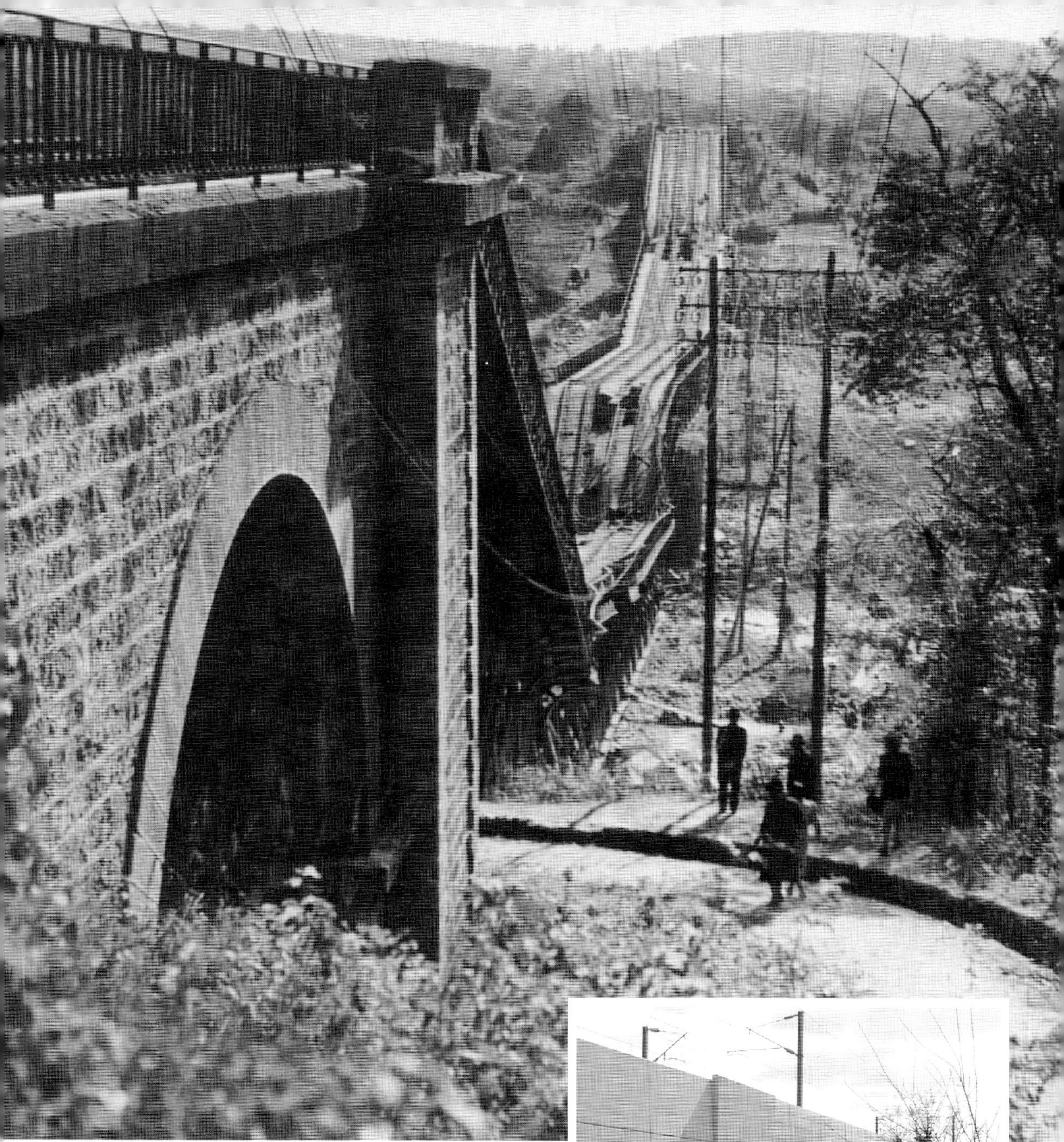

Shortly before 10 p.m. on August 24, a huge explosion had rocked Saint-Germain as the last-remaining Germans blew the Saint-Léger railway viaduct. A few days after liberation, Maurice Veillon went to photograph the impressive wreckage. Grown-up trees and a rebuilt bridge make an exact comparison difficult in Rue du Chemin Vert today.

With the Germans gone and none of the liberators having yet reached the city, August 25 passed eerie and quietly. Here a party of Resistance fighters walk past the Gramont barracks which they had occupied that morning. Rue du Maréchal Lyautey, with buildings of the former barracks, now apartment flats, still lining the street. (M. Veillon and ATB)

One Panther of Kampfgruppe Schweickart had broken down and was left behind Avenue Gambetta. (M. Veillon and ATB)

On August 26, the leaders of the US 5th Armored Division reached Saint-Germain-en-Laye.

Maurice Veillon photographed an M5 light tank reconnoitring the main square situated in front of the château. This is now Place Charles de Gaulle, with, in the background, the chapel at the southern corner of the château.
(M. Veillon)

The population was soon lining the street to cheer the endless American columns that were now crossing the city. Rue de Poissy, pictured in April 2008, with the Post Office in right background.

The ecstatic people of Saint-Germain were standing several deep along Rue du Vieux Marché. The Jeep is approaching from the Rue de Poissy, the street seen in the centre photos. A corner of France where time has stood still.

Displaying makeshift American and British flags on a Citroën. Place Charles de Gaulle, with the château off the picture to the left.

Some days later, units of the French 2ème Division Blindée were quartered in the Gramont barracks and the streets of Saint-Germain were to witness yet another victory parade. To get a better view, the photographer climbed on the remains of the barricade on Rue de Paris. A conveniently situated junction-box allowed us to achieve this perfect comparison.

The Germans having left, a resident examines with curiosity the fortifications erected in the city. This barrier of rails in front of two pillboxes (seen in the background) was part of the elaborate defence system which the Germans had built early during the occupation to protect their quarters against an enemy attack. Rue de Bellevue at its juncture with Rue Félicien David. The two bunkers have gone but another remains a short distance behind the photographer.

In contrast, this barricade blocking the main, southern entrance to the city from the park was one of the makeshift obstacles hastily built during the last days of the German presence in Saint-Germain. Still unaltered after the passing of 65 years, Avenue Le Nôtre opens on the magnificent park in front of the château.

THE OB. WEST BUNKERS

AFTER THE WAR, THE FRENCH authorities set up the Commission de Classement des Ouvrages Militaires to draw up a list of all the defence works built in France during the war, mostly by the Germans, in order to assess their value in the interests of national defence. The local Army Engineers Directorates were responsible for surveying and preparing reports, these files then being submitted to the commission. Each file usually included a detailed plan for each construction and the declared wishes of the local authorities, civilian and military, as to their future use.

After reviewing the reports, the commission sorted the defensive works into three classes. First were those that would be of interest to the Army or another service – they would be taken into official ownership. Second were

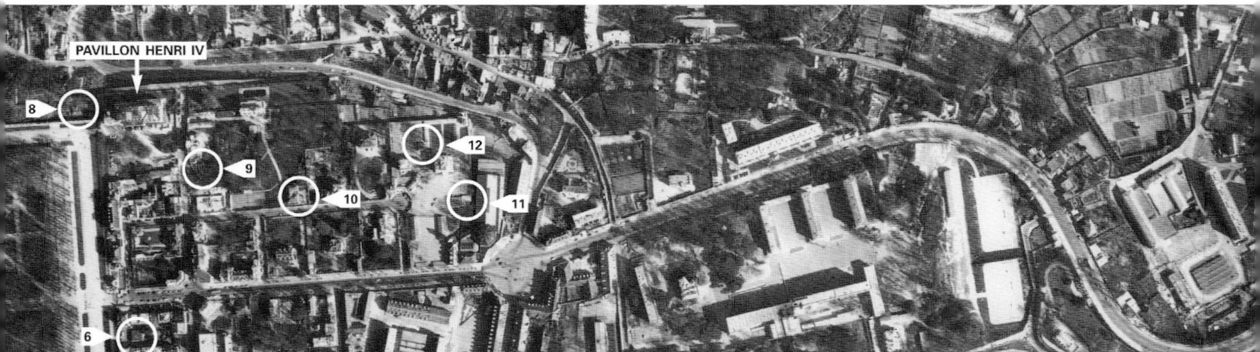

THE OB. WEST BUNKERS AT SAINT-GERMAIN-EN-LAYE

	Code	*Location*	*Size (external)*	*Type*	*Roof*	*Wall*	*Fate*
1	SO-68	MG blockhouse, Place Berteaux	about 10 m²		0.65	0.7	removed 1954
2	SO-145	MG blockhouse, Rue Diderot	about 10 m²		0.65	0.7	removed
3	SO-144	MG blockhouse, 4 rue Félicien David	about 10 m²		0.65	0.7	
4	SO-149	MG blockhouse, 13 rue des Monts Grevets	about 10 m²		0.65	0.7	
5	SO-67	Shelter, Quartier Gramont	18 × 17.5		2	2.5	
6	SO-70	Shelter, Cité Médicis	12.6 × 11.5	Type 622	2	2	
7	SO-69	Shelter, Parc du Château	12.6 × 11.5	Type 622	2	2	
8	SO-71	Underground shelter, Pavillon Henri IV	about 115 m² inside		0.8	0.8	
9	SO-72	Shelter, 16 ter rue Thiers	6.5 × 6		1.5	1.5	removed 1962
10	SO-73	Shelter, 1 rue Salomon Reinach	20 × 11.5		2	2	removed 1983
11	SO-74	Shelter, Saint Erembert School	13.8 × 11.15		2	2	removed 1982
12	SO-75	Shelter, Saint Erembert School	7.65 × 7.65	Type 682	2	1.5	removed 1987
13	SO-64	Underground shelter, Collège Marcel Roby	about 13 m² inside	Type 668	2	1.5	
14	SO-66	Shelter, 25 rue Alexandre Dumas	12.6 × 11.5	Type 622	2	2	
15		Underground shelter, rue Alexandre Dumas	about 80 m² inside				cave filled in 1962
16	SO-61	Shelter, Lycée Jeanne d'Albret	9.8 × 9.6	Type 621	2	2	
17	SO-62	Shelter, Lycée Jeanne d'Albret	12.6 × 11.5	Type 622	2	2	
18	SO-63	Shelter, Lycée Jeanne d'Albret	12.6 × 11.5	Type 622	2	2	
19	SO-65	Headquarters, rue Félicien David	about 1000 m² inside		3	2	
20	SO-60	Shelter, 13 boulevard Victor Hugo	12.6 × 11.5	Type 622	2	2	now a garage
	SO-150	Shelter, Collège Marcel Roby	7.65 × 7.65	Type 668	2	1.5	
	SO-151	Shelter, 12 rue Félicien David	9.8 × 9.6	Type 621	2	2	house built on top

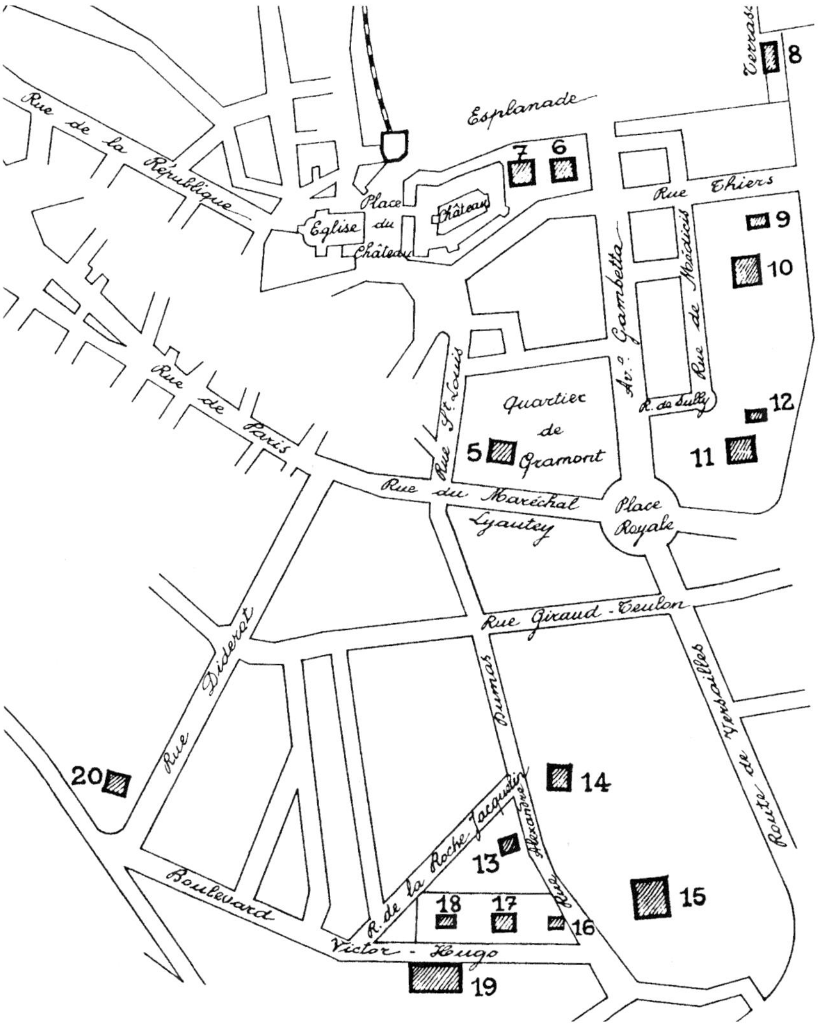

The French Army commission had listed the smaller of the two bunkers at the Saint-Érembert School as No. 11 and the larger one as No. 12 but the engineers who drew up this plan in 1948 switched the numbers by mistake. For clarity's sake, we have corrected the plan.

those that could be handed over to the owner of the land on which they were built but with the proviso that the object would not be demolished. Third were those that could simply be abandoned, leaving the owners free to do what they wanted.

At Saint-Germain-en-Laye, where the bunkers and installations built by the Germans for their Ob. West headquarters were many, it was not until 1947 that the Engineers Directorate based at Versailles had completed their investigation including 22 of them at Saint-Germain. The various proposals for the constructions in the Seine-et-Oise department were considered in June 1948. The Commission studied the future of 20 bunkers at Saint-Germain, re-numbering them 1 to 20, but, for some unexplained reason, they omitted some bunkers in the engineers' files (for example SO-150 and SO-151, which we have included because they still exist today).

To facilitate their description, we have divided the bunkers into four categories.

CONCRETE SHELTERS

Of the 14 surface shelters in Saint-Germain that we know of, most are common types as defined in the Regelbau listing. (The Germans designed all sorts of bunkers, each with a specific purpose varying from infantry shelters and machine-gun posts to command, hospital, and radar bunkers, each being identified by a unique number, and by the end of the war there were about 700 different types in the Regelbau listing.)

The most-common construction found at Saint-Germain was Type 622 (12.60 metres by 11.50 metres), of which there were six, and Type 621 (9.80 metres by 9.60 metres), of which two were built. Both types were personnel shelters with a roof and walls two metres thick, all of reinforced concrete. Type 622 provided two rooms, Type 621 only one. Both had two entrances with a three-centimetre-thick steel door, doubling as an airlock, covered by a small-arms embrasure.

Three of these bunkers stood in the yard of a school, the then Lycée de Jeunes Filles, and, even as the Commission was considering their future, the school's director was insisting that all of them be razed to the ground. The destruction of the roof of one of these bunkers, No. 18, had already begun but the work had been stopped because of lack of funds. Finally, in spite of the protestations of the director, the Commission decided to maintain Nos. 16 and 17.

Eight of these shelters still stand today: No. 6 in the middle of the Cité Médicis near the Château; No. 7 by the side of the Château; No. 14 in Rue Alexandre Dumas; Nos. 16, 17 and 18 in the yard of the Collège Marcel Roby and Lycée Jeanne d'Albret (the old Lycée de Jeunes Filles having since been split into two schools); No. 20, today fitted out as a garage with an entrance three metres wide and two metres high cut through the front facing the Boulevard Victor Hugo; and SO-151 in the Rue Félicien David on which a house has now been built.

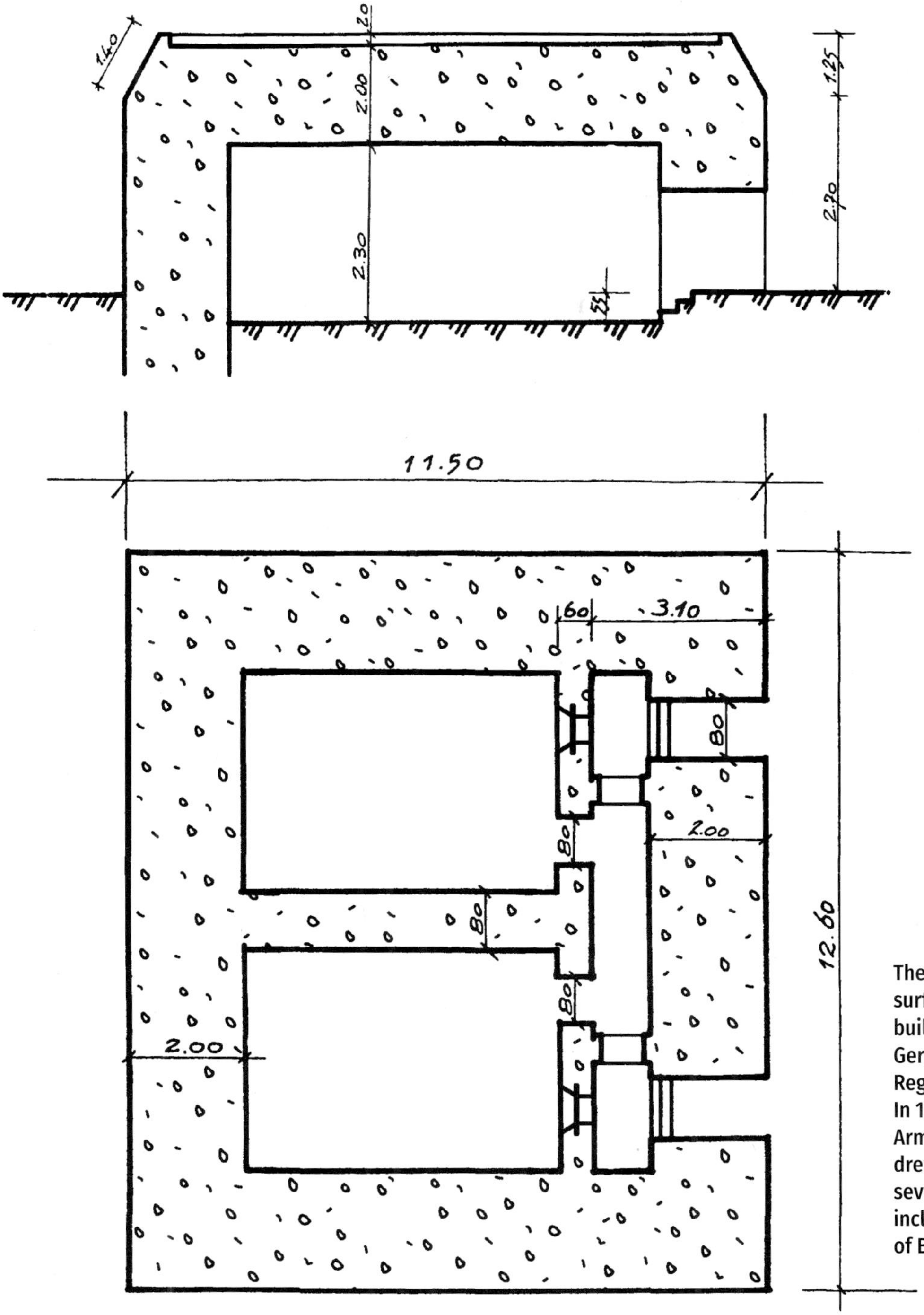

The most-common surface shelter built at Saint-Germain was Regelbau Type 622. In 1947 the French Army engineers drew plans of several of them, including this one of Bunker No. 6.

The second group consists of three larger shelters of different sizes and shapes. They were not of a standardised Regelbau type but were each of a special design (Sonderkonstruktion).

Bunker No. 5, standing in the yard of the Gramont barracks, measured about 18 by 17.5 metres. Its two main rooms provided over 150 square metres of useful space under a two-metre-thick roof slab. The outer walls were 2.5

Two of the six surviving Types 622 stand in the yard of the Collège Marcel Roby and Lycée Jeanne d'Albret, Bunkers No. 17 and No. 18. Destruction of No. 18 began just after the war but the work stopped due to lack of funds after about half a metre of the concrete roof had been removed.

Type 622 was basically designed as a two-group accommodation shelter (Doppelgruppenunterstand) for 20 men, with bunks and tables, heating, lighting, and amenities. When used, as at Saint-Germain, as simple bomb-proof shelters the facilities were not all installed and the space thus gained enlarged the shelter's capacity to about 50 men. Bunker No. 7 located in the château park can be easily accessed.

metres thick and machine-gun embrasures covered its three entrances (two at one end and one at the opposite end). Most likely it housed one of the Ob. West telephone exchanges.

Bunker No. 10, located in a private estate along the Rue Médicis (today the Rue Salomon Reinach), measured 20 by 13.6 metres. No plan seems to have survived, so it is not known how the interior of about 150 square metres was laid out.

The 90-degree turn at the entrance (to the left here as it is the right-hand entry) and the small-arms embrasure that protected it.

One of the armoured doors of Bunker No. 7. Each of the two entrances had one such door, forming an airlock in between. Regular Regelbau doors, they were 30mm thick, of the stable-door type, with a rubber seal around the rim to make them gas-tight. This is the one that closes the entrance after the 90-degree, seen from inside the airlock.

Many of the bunker walls are adorned with inscriptions. In most cases they are instructions or warnings but one also finds Nazi insignia, zealous exhortations of courage or, like here in Bunker No. 7, artistic attempts by homesick soldiers.

Bunker No. 11, in the grounds of the Saint-Érembert School, measured 13.80 by 11.15 metres (excluding the porch that protected each of the two entrances) and its one main room provided about 60 square metres of space. The roof and walls were two metres thick. It may have been a communications centre.

The Commission proposed to preserve these three large bunkers, noting that No. 5 was then being used to house prisoners and store ammunition, and that the proprietor of No. 10 had already built a house on top of it, having converted the bunker itself into a garage.

Bunkers No. 10 and 11 were demolished in the early 1980s, but No. 5 survives to this day. The Gramont barracks were used by the Army until the late 1990s, their last use of No. 5 being to stock up ammunition in one room and wine for the officers' mess in the other. The former barracks have since been converted into apartment flats and bunker No. 5 now serves mainly as a parking space for bicycles and baby prams.

Just 50 metres from Bunker No. 7, Bunker No. 6, another Type 622, still stands today in the middle of the Cité Médicis. It is a real nuisance in such a small space but until today, the colossal work required for its destruction has discouraged any plans to remove it.

This plan was drawn in 1947 by the French Army engineers of Bunker No. 12 which was located in the grounds of the Saint-Érembert School but has since been demolished. In German terminology it was a Regelbau Type 682 designed to house a power generator which makes sense as it stood close to bunker No. 11 housing communications equipment. Bunker No. 11 was demolished in 1982.

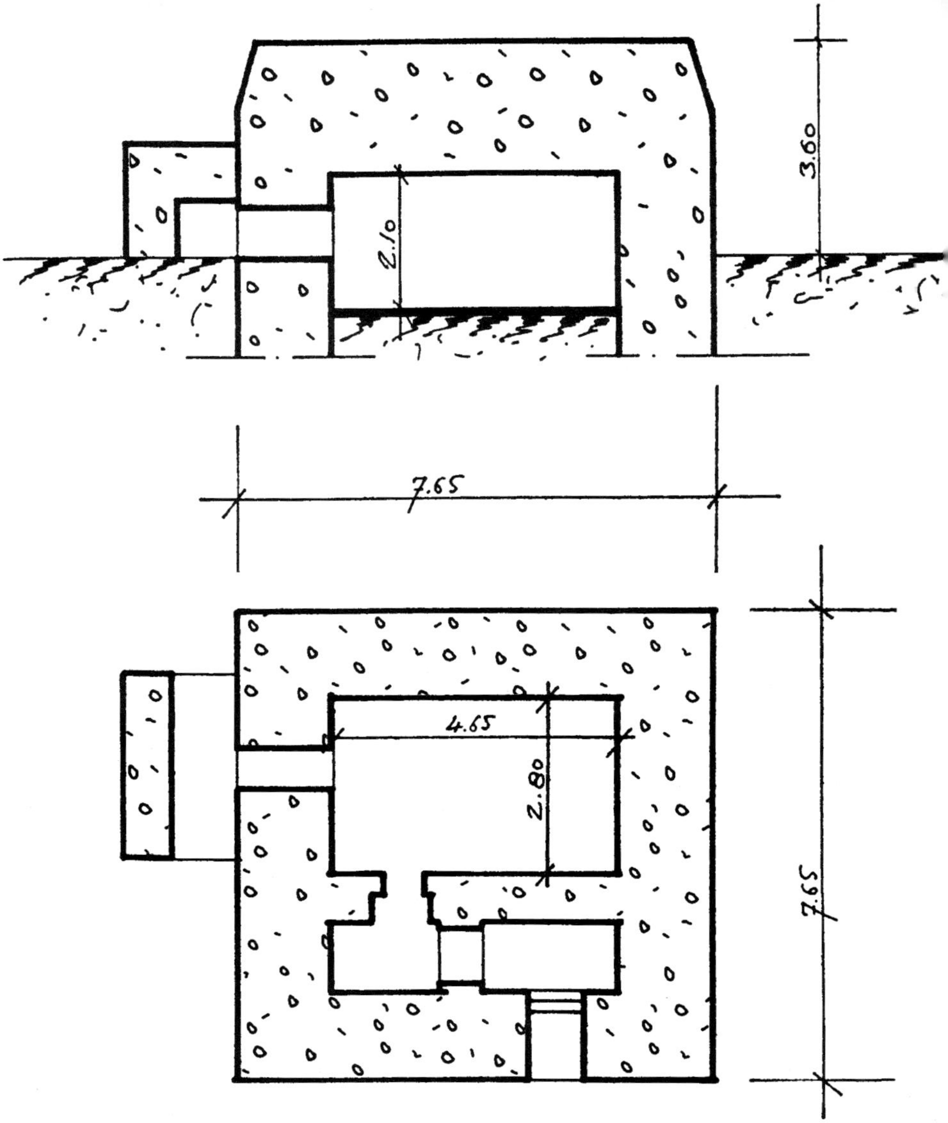

Travelling down Boulevard Victor Hugo from east to west today, four bunkers stand on the right-hand side of the street, Nos. 16, 17, 18 and SO-150 in that order. A few days after the liberation, Maurice Veillon photographed the last of these four, the then pristine SO-150. Little of the bunker can be seen today from the street. (M. Veillon and ATB)

The third batch of concrete shelters comprises three smaller bunkers featuring only one room and a single entrance. Two of them measured 7.65 by 7.65 metres and had a two-metre-thick roof but walls only 1.5 metres thick. No. 12 located in the grounds of the Saint-Érembert School was a Regelbau Type 682, designed to house a power generator – which makes sense as it stood close to bunker No. 11, a larger construction housing communications equipment. SO-150, built in the grounds of the Lycée de Jeunes Filles, was a

This is SO-150 as it looks today, photographed from the grounds of the Lycée Jeanne d'Albret. It is a Type 668 denoting a small shelter for six men (Kleinstunterstand für 6 Mann).

Bunker No. 16 as it looks today in the Lycée Jeanne d'Albret. In German terminology it was a Regelbau Type 621 designed as a one-group accommodation shelter for 10 men.

Measuring 18 metres by 17.5 metres, with a roof 2 metres thick, the largest of the shelters was bunker No. SO-67 in the courtyard of the Gramont barracks. Apartments now occupy the buildings of the former barracks and the bunker stands in the park in the centre of the residence.

Type 668, a small shelter for six men. No. 9, along Rue Thiers, measured 6.5 by 6 metres and had a roof and walls both 1.5 metres thick. No plan of it seems to have survived and doubt remains as to its function.

Although the Commission proposed to preserve Nos. 9 and 12, only the third bunker, SO-150, survived. It still stands in the grounds of the present-day Lycée Jeanne d'Albret.

The story of the pair of bunkers, Nos. 11 and 12, in the grounds of the Saint-Érembert School gives an indication of the difficulties encountered in living with such massive constructions in one's back yard. In October 1966, the school finally obtained permission to demolish them but it was not until 1982 that it was able to fund the destruction of No. 11 (which until then had been used as a changing-room for when the pupils played sport in the nearby yard, the art teacher having painted it in bright colours to render it less ugly). Explosives could not be used due to the proximity of the school buildings so the contractor who dealt with it during the summer holidays could only use pneumatic drills. However, it soon became apparent that he had badly

Another Type 621, Bunker SO-151 is still located at 12 Rue Félicien David. The bunker measures 9.8 metres by 9.6 metres, with walls and a roof 2 metres thick, and a house is built on top.

At the junction of Rue Alexandre Dumas and Rue de la Rochejaquelein, Bunker No. 14, another Type 622, is now nicely engulfed in a bush so thick that no passer-by can imagine that there is a large bunker there.

under-estimated the strength of the reinforced concrete and the operation lasted much longer than anticipated, the contractor losing heavily on the contract. Bunker No. 12, lying some 25 metres away and hidden by trees, survived for a few years longer, and was finally removed in the summer of 1987.

UNDERGROUND INSTALLATIONS

Three of the works studied by the Commission were underground constructions. The first, No. 8, was a shelter built under the terrace near the Pavillon Henri IV, where the Ob. West headquarters had first been installed. Measuring over 20 metres in length and 6 in width, the bunker was divided into three large rooms. Its roof was less than a metre thick, causing the Commission to note that it would only have been proof against shrapnel. They considered it of no interest and proposed to abandon

The underground shelter close to the Pavillon Henri IV (No. 8) was one of the first to be built at Saint-Germain. Being an early creation, it was not a standardised 'Regelbau' construction. Its concrete roof was only 80 centimetres thick — not even proof against a direct 150mm shell.

The French Army commission charged with assessing wartime German defence works after the war declared it of no interest. However, its position right next to the Pavillon Henri IV did not allow it to be removed without risk and the underground bunker remains today, with these well-preserved urinals.

it after the equipment inside, including two hand-operated air ventilators, had been recovered.

A second underground installation, No. 15, was a rock cave, about 16 metres long and 5 metres wide. German engineers had consolidated the ceiling with concrete and installed two armoured doors. The Commission proposed to preserve the cave as it was, but in 1962, it was filled in.

The third underground construction, No. 13, had been the personnel shelter for von Rundstedt. It lay in the garden of the villa where he had lived for three years in the grounds of the Lycée de Jeunes Filles. (Originally, there had only been a makeshift shelter in the existing cellar of the villa, iron and plating having been used to strengthen its walls and ceiling. This shelter was quite small, only about five

Remarkably, the two underground shelters built for von Rundstedt can both still be seen at the Villa David: the makeshift 'iron' construction in the cellar, and the Type 668 shelter built under the garden. The air-purification equipment remains in perfect condition in the cellar. A Type HES 0,6 (0.6 standing for the volume of air, in cubic metres, it could ventilate per minute), it is said to be the only one of this type known to survive.

A ten-metre-long passage leads from the basement of the villa to the Type 668 shelter. Colonel Henri de Rolland, local historian, guided us along with torches.

The garden shelter was fitted out with more-powerful ventilation equipment, a Type HES 1,2 (purifying 1.2 cubic metres of air per minute).

The entrance area of the garden shelter still features the original electrical equipment. The circular item seen upper left is the Überdrückventil (high pressure valve) which adjusted air pressure inside the shelter if the ventilation equipment created an over-pressure.

The standardised Notausgang (emergency exit) with the steel girders that were built in to strengthen this weak spot in the bunker wall. This shelter was additionally provided with an escape staircase starting from the tunnel as it reaches the bunker.

square metres. The Commission did not allocate it a number.) The bunker constructed under the garden was connected to the villa by a tunnel about ten metres long. It was a Regelbau Type 668, but with an additional dividing wall, probably built to provide some private quarters for the Field-Marshal. The interior measured about 13 square metres, the two main rooms each being about five metres square. It had wood panelling on all the walls and ceiling, ventilation equipment and a stove, and was provided with three beds.

In 1948, the Commission noted that the bunker was still in perfect condition and proposed to preserve it as it was. In July 1949 there occurred a mix-up between the 'von Rundstedt villa' (No. 13) and the 'von Rundstedt bunker' (which referred to No. 19, the huge Ob. West command bunker – see below), the authorities by mistake earmarking the bunker in the villa garden for handing over to the French Air Force. However, the error was soon rectified and instead the villa and its underground bunker were handed over to the school in whose grounds it stood (then the Lycée de Jeunes Filles, now part of the Collège Marcel Roby). Both the small makeshift shelter in the cellar and the Type 668 under the garden remain in a remarkable state of repair, including their ventilation equipment, although lacking proper maintenance. Closed with concrete slabs the two emergency exits are still there under the playground.

MAIN OB. WEST HEADQUARTERS

The main Ob. West headquarters bunker – No. 19 for the Commission – had been built in front of an ancient quarry and the German engineers made use of some old cavities in the rock. The building comprised three blocks, two with two floors and the other with only one. It measured over 60 metres in length but its actual size is not easy to determine for it follows the shape of the hillside against which it is built. The building contained about 40 rooms, or over 60 if passages, corridors, and toilets are taken into account as some old German numbering faintly visible inside the bunker runs up to 63. The Commission reported that the thickness of the concrete wall was two metres

No photo, outside or inside, has ever surfaced showing the main Ob. West headquarters bunker during the war. One can understand that the Germans banned all photography for security reasons but, at the same time, one might assume that in the summer of 1944 American or British intelligence teams would have been tasked to investigate and photograph what was, after all, the former command post of the German High Command in the West. Nevertheless, no such survey appears to have been carried out. The huge bunker today falls under the responsibility of the Musée d'Archéologie at the Saint-Germain château. Unfortunately, it can not be entered due to safety restrictions and the outside area is also strictly off limits.

and that of the roof three metres. The Versailles Engineers believed that 100,000 tonnes of concrete had been used to build the bunker. One non-documented account indicates that the construction took eight months, with three 400-man teams working day and night on eight-hour shifts, while another source gives 15 months.

In the centre, the main part of the complex had two levels with a total area of about 500 square metres. The lower level provided the bunker's two entrances with two interior staircases giving access to the upper level. One wing of the upper level consisted of an annex block of 160 square metres, with a second floor above of similar size. The second wing, on the left behind the main block and on a higher level, comprised another annex block of some 150 square metres. About one hundred metres away, by the side of the bunker access stood a single-storey brick building, 45 by 15 metres, providing additional office spaces.

The Commission reported that the main bunker was in good condition although some parts were damp (not surprising for there had been no ventilation for months), and they proposed to retain it. However, the

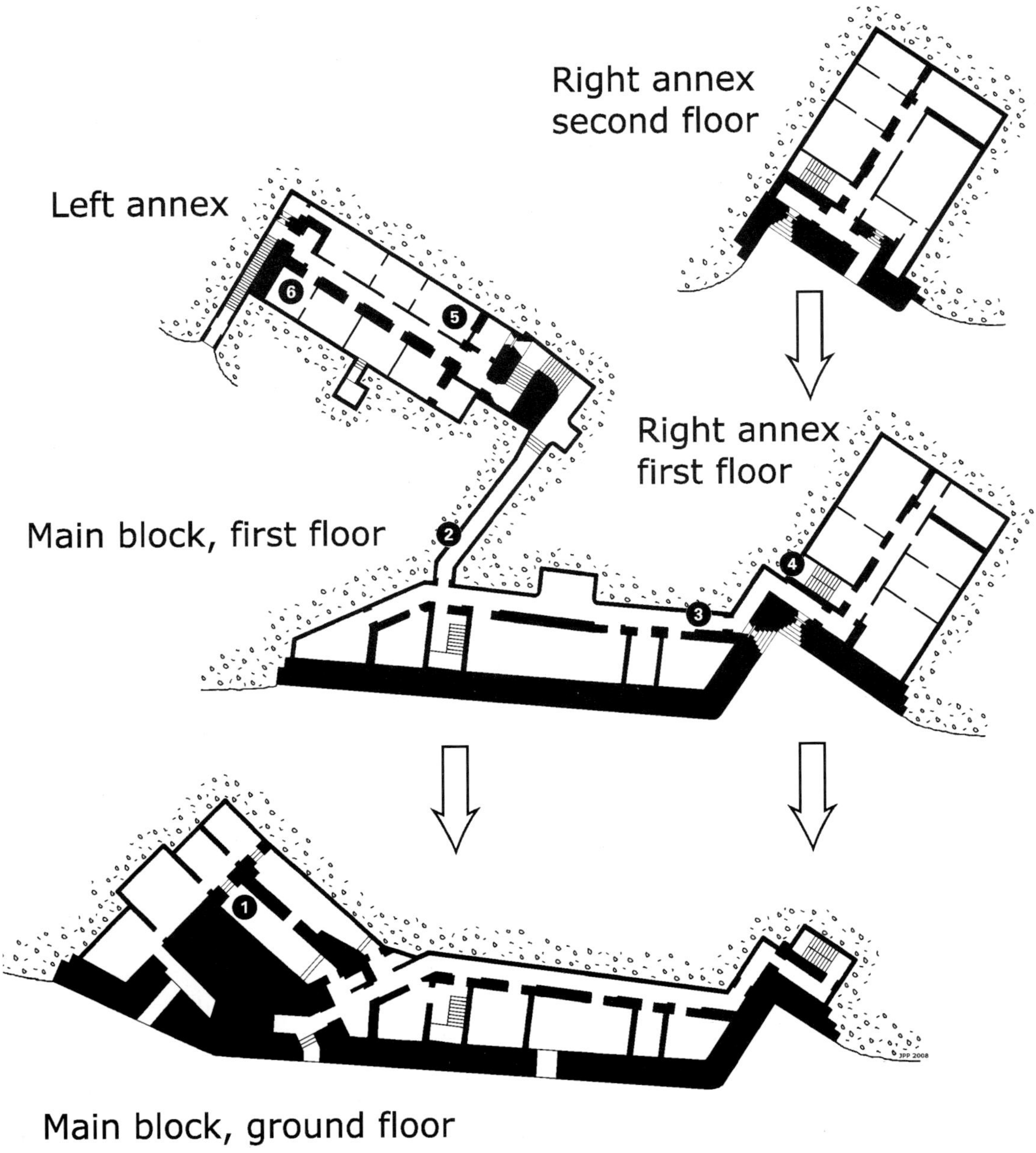

The headquarters bunker comprised a main block with two floors, an annex on the right, also with two floors, and an annex on the left with only one storey. No original German plan of this massive construction appears to have survived. This basic plan therefore is a composite of those drawn long after the war by the French new owners, supplemented with the invaluable information from Pierre Vidalainq's sketches, the young scout who surveyed the whole installation in May 1945. His drawings and associated report give details that would otherwise have been lost, particularly about all the interior walls that were removed after the war to provide larger rooms. On all floors of the two annex blocks, the brick walls that were along the right-hand side of the corridors (seen from the staircase) have been demolished, as have the walls separating the rooms on both sides of the corridors. The number of rooms on each side varied, being either two, three or four. The walls on the corridor side were about 20 centimetres thick and those dividing the rooms about 15 centimetres. The whole building provided about 40 rooms or over 60 if passages, corridors, and toilets are included. (Some old German numbering faintly visible in the left-hand annex include '46' and '49' and numbers in the right-hand annex go up to 63.) This plan does not include the doors nor show all the details of the kitchens, washrooms and toilets, etc. The thickness of the concrete walls against the rock can only be indicative.

Three machine-gun embrasures, positioned at the junction of the main block and the right-hand annex block of the bunker, covered its outside approaches. Two of them, placed at right angle from each other, were operated from the first-floor corridor.

brick building was in poor shape and had been thoroughly looted so the Commission decided that it should be abandoned.

After considering the Commission's findings, in mid-1949 the Armée de l'Air declared its intention of using the bunker for a new Air Defence central command post. The bunker and 8,000 square metres of land was bought by the State but, after looking into things more closely, the air force concluded that it would be unwise to install modern equipment in the old bunker, and in January 1953 officially discarded the idea.

When the Ministère de la Culture made noises that they were looking for a repository for art treasures in case of war, and had their eye on the Ob. West headquarters block, the air force had second thoughts about handing it over. A new study was commissioned but it reached the same conclusion, namely that it would be impractical to install the piping and cabling for electricity,

The third firing-slit was on the second level of the annex block, just above the one seen on the right in the other picture. The outside of the embrasures was shaped as an inverted step-pyramid to prevent ricochets from entering the bunker.

heating, and ventilation necessary for a modern command post through thick reinforced concrete. As the bunker was located in a residential area, close to a school, the report also concluded: ‘it does not appear sensible to make it a highly interesting target for enemy aviation’.

All plans to use the bunker for military purposes were finally abandoned in July 1954 whereupon the Ministère de la Culture renewed its request to have the complex allocated to them for storage of art treasures. The former Ob. West bunker was turned over to them in March 1955.

No plan of the massive bunker appears to have survived, neither architectural blueprints from the Organisation Todt that built it nor functional sketches by the Ob. West services that used it. Luckily, in 1945, in order to gain his Boy Scout topographic certificate, a local teenager, 17-year-old Pierre Vidalainq, was sent to survey the bunker. On May 19 he was led into the huge construction by Miss Brisson who was quite familiar with the place as she lived nearby. There was no lighting working inside and the whole survey visit was carried out just with torches. Pierre’s report and sketches are amazingly detailed and they have given us much valuable information that would otherwise have been lost forever. Although the bunker had been thoroughly looted and virtually nothing remained of the furniture or technical equipment, he was still able to describe the functions of each room, the ventilation and telephone installations, the barrack rooms, and the High Command quarters. Even more importantly,

The Musée d'Archéologie uses the former German headquarters bunker to store original moulds of statues, particularly from the Napoléon III period. According to young Pierre Vidalainq, this room in the left-hand part of the basement (see plan, position [1]) was a billet for troops. It was built in the rock cavities of the ancient quarry, hence the vaulted ceiling with a height of about 4.8 metres (in the rest of the construction, the ceiling height is about 2.5 metres).

his sketches showed all the dividing walls that have since been removed.

'A few steps down', noted Pierre, 'and we enter the building. The temperature is suddenly colder by several degrees, a shiver goes down my back.'

The basement of the main central block provides the bunker's two entrances and two interior stairways give access to the upper levels. One staircase is about two metres wide, the other 1.70 metres. Not including passages and corridors, the useful space in the basement is 12 rooms. In the left-hand part, the German engineers had made use of rock cavities from the ancient quarry and concreted them. The apex of the vaulted ceiling in these rooms is about 4.8 metres high whereas in the rest of the construction the ceiling is about 2.5 metres high.

The gallery leading to the upper left block, as seen from position [2]. In May 1945, Pierre Vidalainq reported an iron gate sealing the access to the gallery but this has now disappeared (it would have stood just behind the photographer's position).

The corridor on the first floor of the main block, seen from position [3] at the turn leading to the right-hand annex. Young Pierre wrote that he saw a considerable amount of machinery and numerous large pipes penetrating the ceiling in the row of rooms on the left. The nearest door leads to the room that housed an air-purification plant, the second to what was the technical crew quarters and the third to the large space that accommodated the ventilation equipment.

A machine-gun embrasure on the first floor, featuring the standard Stahlschartenplatte (armoured plate with loophole and observation slit) measuring 1.4 x 0.75 metres.

According to Pierre, the left part of the basement was fitted out as a barracks, with four accommodation rooms and two ablution rooms with toilets, washbasins, and showers. 'The beds, a metal frame with mesh, were anchored to the walls by two rings and suspended to the roof by chains.'

Walking from the staircase along the 25-metre-long corridor, Pierre described the series of rooms on the right-hand side. The first contained a water tank that took up half the room, then came the main electrical installation chamber. This measured about 26 square metres and was one of the largest rooms in the complex. 'The equipment that was in the middle of the room has been blown, only its plinth remains. On the left-hand side there are three alcoves with one intact transformer.'

The next room was the technical crew quarters with the boiler in the last room before the turn of the corridor. 'The fortress had a central heating', wrote Pierre, 'but sadly all radiators have been removed. As the visit to this floor is now complete, we keep along the corridor and take the staircase that leads to the first floor. It is a little warmer here.'

The first floor of the central block had five rooms on one side of the corridor with a recess on the other side that might well have been for sleeping accommodation because of the fittings which remain to be seen. The room at the end of the corridor was the sick bay (its walls and floor still nicely tiled today) with toilets and washbasins in the adjacent room. Walking back down the corridor and passing the staircase, there was a large room about 45 square metres (the largest room in the complex) housing the powerful ventilation equipment, then the technical crew quarters and another room with air-purification plant. Pierre described 'much machinery and numerous large pipes going through the ceiling'. On the wall on the side of the corridor there were 'numerous metres distributing the air to the various rooms, each with two handles that enabled to control the flow of air'. In each room, Pierre saw how the pipe bringing fresh air was 'either hanging from the ceiling or fastened on the wall', with a grill near the floor on the opposite corner for the extraction. The system effectively renewed the air throughout the whole bunker, avoiding condensation, while the internal pressure secured it against a gas attack. Unfortunately, all the pipework which Pierre describes no longer remains.

At the end of the block, the corridor ended in two successive 90-degree turns before reaching the second staircase. In the right-hand side wall, two machine-gun embrasures were provided to cover the outside approaches to the bunker.

Passing the staircase, Pierre describes reaching an iron gate giving access to the annex block that he identified as the communications centre. Before the gate was a sign near a button: 'KLINGEL ZUM VERMITTLUNGSBETRIEB' (Ring to Communications Centre).

The corridor which ran along the whole length of this block contained two rooms on the left and four on the right. The first room on the left appeared to have been the male staff quarters and the second the telex room measuring about 25 square metres. Pierre noted with surprise that a 'nice chandelier' was still hanging from its ceiling. On the right-hand side of the corridor lay first the telephone room with 'a mass of cables lying all around', then the female staff room, followed by another with telex equipment, and finally a kitchen, toilets, and washbasins.

Pierre then retraced his steps 'to the staircase from where we came but this time we climbed to the second floor where it was much warmer. Here we entered the rooms of the high commanders, the walls of which were covered with wood panelling giving the impression of being in ship cabins'. Though Pierre labelled all these rooms as Superior Officer apartments, it seems probable however that some were in fact offices and map rooms.

As on the lower level, a corridor ran the whole length of the block, but here with three rooms on the left and two on the right, plus a guardroom at the entrance.

The first room on the left still contained a washbasin and cupboard, while at the far end a nicely-panelled suite, about 15 square metres in all, was designed for the Commander-in-Chief. On the other side of the corridor was another large room with a washbasin and cupboard, and more toilet and washing facilities lay at the far end of the corridor.

Two apertures had been provided in the front wall of the bunker (the other three sides being underground), one being a machine-gun embrasure (just above the same one at the lower level) and the other a narrow entrance. In between was a sloping pipe about 20 centimetres in diameter to enable those inside to drop grenades onto an attacker at the bottom of the wall. Two successive iron gates blocked the entrance access and, from a room in front of the staircase, a machine-gun embrasure covered the short corridor to the entrance. Outside a double ladder gave access to the main platform in front of the bunker. (This appears to have been some sort of arrangement providing a short-cut to the senior officer's apartments, which seemed to be of a removable type with hooks.)

Somewhat behind the left-hand side of the main bunker, and on a higher level, was a second annex block of six main rooms. According to what Pierre heard in 1945, this had been the last part of the complex to be built, after the first part was completed and in operation.

Starting from the first floor of the main block, through another iron gate that sealed access, a long gallery led to a U-shaped stairway protected by another gate and defended by a machine-gun embrasure. From the top of the stairway another sloping pipe enabled grenades to be dropped into the gallery below.

Pierre said that there was no equipment remaining in any of the rooms that ran off the corridor (three on each side), apart from some cupboards, and it seems that this was the office part of the bunker. In the larger room on the left-hand side, an iron gate covered a shaft venting through a chimney on the roof. At the far end of the corridor, behind more armoured doors, a long emergency staircase led to an escape door exiting in the wood above

Being one of the largest rooms to be found in the bunker today, this space in the left annex as seen from position [5] is often mistakenly presented as the 'map room'. There were actually three much-smaller rooms here in German times before the dividing brick walls were pulled down. The centre door in the background leads to the bunker's escape stairway, the one on the right to the machine gun position covering it.

The adjoining room, equally spacious and often referred to as another 'map room', was also originally divided up into three smaller rooms (position [6]).

the bunker. A narrow room at the corner of the block with a machine-gun embrasure covered the whole length of the stairs.

'Up the stairs we emerge into fresh air', wrote Pierre after his exploration tour.' We are on the roof of the fortress. Weeds grow all around in between some ventilation chimneys.'

DEFENCE BUNKERS

The small defensive bunkers that the Germans had built in and around Saint-Germain were of little interest. There were too many to justify individual study and form-filing so the engineers listed only a few examples, omitting the one at Place Édouard Detaille, since demolished, and the two-storey bunker that still exists at 6bis Boulevard Victor Hugo.

The first four constructions studied by the Commission, numbered 1 to 4, were small machine-gun bunkers built at key points to cover streets from their firing slits. About 6 to 10 square metres in size, they were considered of no interest and the commission proposed to abandon them. They were a nuisance to road traffic and two were already in the process of being destroyed (No. 1 by the side of Place Berteaux and No. 2 in the Rue Diderot) but the other two (No. 3 – Rue Félicien David and No. 4 – Rue des Monts Grevets) have survived to the present day.

Although there were numerous pillboxes in Saint-Germain, the French commission set up to evaluate all the German fortifications as to their future usefulness, surveyed only four of them. This is No. 1 beside what was then Place Berteaux. It was demolished in September 1954 but the château provides with a nice background for his comparison.

One of those pillboxes not surveyed by the French Army Commission was this one Place Édouard Detaille. It was removed in the 1950s and no trace of it remains today.

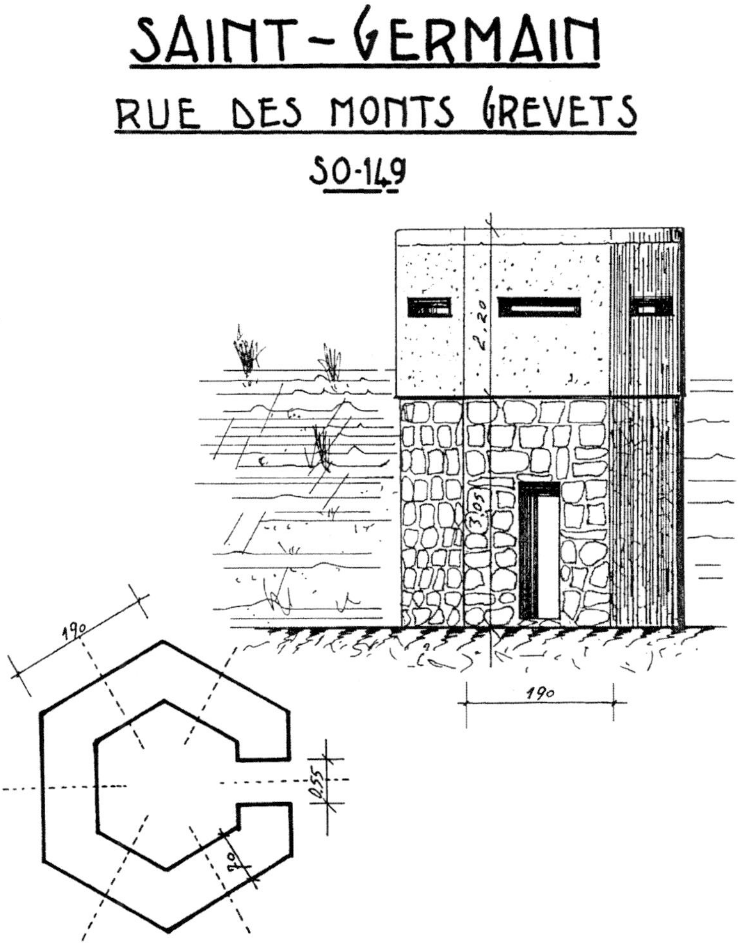

This sketch, drawn by the French Army engineers in 1947, shows the bunker on the Rue des Monts Grevets (No. 4). This featured six machine-gun embrasures covering every approach. It still stands today, virtually unchanged since 1944. In addition to elaborate pillboxes illustrated here, the Germans cut many firing-slits through existing walls all over the city. Several of these can still be seen: in the wall facing the park beside the iron gate of the Pavillon Henri IV, another facing the length of Rue La Rochejaquelein near Bunker No. 14, and a third one covering the curve of the street about No. 11 Rue des Monts Grevets.

Another of the machine-gun bunkers that still exists is this impressive two-storey construction, featuring three embrasures on the lower floor and six on the upper one. For some reason, the French Army commission did not include it in its survey. It is situated in a private property at No. 6 bis Boulevard Victor Hugo and one must not approach it without having first being given permission by the owner.

Bunker No. 3 is another pillbox that has survived. Located at No. 4 Rue Félicien David, it can be easily approached and photographed.

Historian Bruno Renoult traced that a team of the Office of Strategic Services, OSS, had established quarters in Saint-Germain in April 1945. According to the original caption of this photo, Lieutenant J. B. Harris Jr, the commander of 'Areas B-1 and B-2' posed with his staff at Area B-2. This is the rear view of Area B-2.

Remarkably, this American photo of the house they named Area B-1 shows that this was the same villa where the German headquarters of the I. Abteilung of Heeresgruppen-Nachrichten-Regiment 570 was once quartered in 1940 and 1941! See below a snapshot of this same villa from Oberleutnant Robert Lanius's album. (R. Lanius)